ADVANCE PRAISE FOR

TRANSFORMATIVE Cʀɪᴛɪᴄᴀʟ ꜱᴇʀᴠɪᴄᴇ-ʟᴇᴀʀɴɪɴɢ:
THEORY AND PRACTICE FOR ENGAGING COMMUNITY COLLEGE
AND UNIVERSITY LEARNERS IN BUILDING AN ACTIVIST MINDSET

"*Transformative Critical Service-Learning*, by Dr. Heather Coffey and Dr. Lucy Arnold, delivers a theoretical framework and practical strategies for designing, implementing, assessing, and reflecting on critical service-learning experiences. This work is grounded in the theoretical constructs of critical service-learning and incorporates Nicole Mirra's work on critical civic empathy as an impetus for reflection and self-awareness. The authors introduce the Critical Service-Learning Implementation Model (CSLIM) as a tool for critical service-learning design and provide examples of this work to better understand the pragmatics and affordances of implementation. This book is a superb resource for faculty implementing or teaching about critical service-learning."

Barri Tinkler, Ph.D.
Interim Dean and Professor
Missouri State University

"Deeply grounded in the historical roots of critical service-learning - as well as current theory and practice - *Transformative Critical Service-Learning* offers us more than the what and the why - it provides a much-needed map to the how. While much of the existing scholarship on critical service-learning focuses on questions of definition and theory, Coffey and Arnold offer a well-scaffolded guide to what critical service-learning actually looks like in practice in K-12 schools and higher education. Community-engaged scholars, practitioners, teachers, and teacher educators at all levels will benefit from this book. The authors engagingly delineate strategically crafted instructional activities, implementation models, case studies, asset mapping schemes, assessment strategies, and an array of thoughtful tools for effectively implementing critical service-learning. Coffey and Arnold demonstrate a deep commitment to transformative learning - not simply for students, but for faculty, community partners, and all collaborators in critical service-learning experiences. Coffey and Arnold keenly recognize that critical consciousness isn't something that randomly happens – rather, critical consciousness is a heightened level of awareness and action that we can intentionally grow – but only when we create the enabling conditions, spaces, relationships, and deep learning experiences which best foster its development – *Transformative Critical Service-Learning* is a thoughtfully constructed guidebook to the creation of these necessary enabling conditions."

David Malone, Ph.D.
Professor of the Practice of Education
Director of the Service-Learning Program
Duke University

"Heather Coffey and Lucy Arnold have produced an exceptionally readable, researched, and useful book on critical service-learning. This brief, but comprehensive text provides a panoramic guide for becoming a critical service-learning teacher in schools and colleges. Coffey and Arnold invite and equip teachers to embrace service-learning as a pedagogy for democratic social change in education and society. Their panoramic and systematic excursion in the theory and practice of critical service-learning is also a book of love and hope for improving the world. This work is a bright light in dark times."

Ira Shor, Ph.D.
Professor
College of Staten Island

"*Transformative Critical Service-Learning* invites university educators to challenge traditional understandings of both 'service' and 'learning' and reorient their practice toward the design of mutually humanizing partnerships grounded in commitments to equity, empathy, and justice. Coffey and Arnold offer educators the theoretical and practical tools they so urgently need to navigate the social, cultural, and political dimensions (and tensions) of critical service-learning alongside students and communities in ways that foster individual and collective transformation."

Nicole Mirra, Ph.D.
Assistant Professor of Urban Teacher Education
Rutgers University

# TRANSFORMATIVE CRITICAL SERVICE-LEARNING

# TRANSFORMATIVE CRITICAL SERVICE-LEARNING

Theory and Practice for Engaging Community College and University Learners in Building an Activist Mindset

BY HEATHER COFFEY

AND LUCY ARNOLD

Myers
Education
Press

*Gorham, Maine*

Copyright © 2022 | Myers Education Press, LLC
Published by Myers Education Press, LLC
P.O. Box 424
Gorham, ME 04038

**Myers Education Press** is an academic publisher specializing in books, e-books and digital content in the field of education. All of our books are subjected to a rigorous peer review process and produced in compliance with the standards of the Council on Library and Information Resources.

Library of Congress Cataloging-in-Publication Data available from Library of Congress.

13-digit ISBN 978-1-9755-0499-1 (paperback)
13-digit ISBN 978-1-9755-0500-4 (library networkable e-edition)
13-digit ISBN 978-1-9755-0501-1 (consumer e-edition)

Printed in the United States of America.

All first editions printed on acid-free paper that meets the American National Standards Institute Z39-48 standard.

Books published by Myers Education Press may be purchased at special quantity discount rates for groups, workshops, training organizations and classroom usage. Please call our customer service department at 1-800-232-0223 for details.

*Cover design by Teresa Lagrange.*

Visit us on the web at **www.myersedpress.com** to browse our complete list of titles.

## Dedication

To the service-learning students and community partners beside whom we've worked and from whom we've learned

—H and L

# Contents

# Acknowledgments

THERE ARE TOO MANY ACKNOWLEDGMENTS for us to list, but here is a starting place. We want to thank our colleague Dr. Meghan Barnes for keen insights into critical service-learning. We also appreciate Dr. Tania Mitchell, whose work in critical service-learning is seminal, for her thinking and questions at the American Educational Research Association (AERA) 2021 annual meeting. We also acknowledge the members of the Service-Learning and Experiential Education Special Interest Group at AERA who tirelessly work to bring notoriety to this area of teaching and learning. We are beyond appreciative to the team at Myers Education Press for guiding us through this publishing process, especially Chris Myers.

Heather would also like to thank Dr. Kathy Sykes, who gave her the opportunity to teach a service-learning course to undergraduate education minors while earning her doctorate; Dr. Nicole Webster for encouraging her to think more critically about service-learning; and to all the scholars in the field who have challenged her to think about the potential of service-learning as a tool for teacher preparation. Most importantly, Heather is grateful to her husband, Corwin, and her daughters for giving her occasional peace and quiet so she could write this book!

Lucy would also like to thank Gregory Avery-Weir and Melissa Avery-Weir, who have both individually and together listened to her talk through ideas and asked the perfect questions.

She is also grateful to Dr. Malin Pereira and Megan Anderson for encouraging her to teach courses focused on critical service-learning. She also appreciates all the faculty and students who have shared their energy, time, and spaces with her, especially Stephanie Hyman.

# The Work to Make
# Service-Learning Critical

*Tania D. Mitchell, University of Minnesota*

---

I FIRST ENCOUNTERED SERVICE-LEARNING AS AN undergraduate student. It was an "innovative pedagogical experiment" that gave students, like me, the opportunity to exchange a research paper for 20 hours of service in a local community organization. As a first-year, first-generation college student, I found service-learning transformative. It altered my experiences as a student, deepened my sense of connection to the city where I went to school, and shifted my expectations for "what kind of citizen," to borrow a phrase from Westheimer and Kahne (2004), I would become. After that course in my first year, I spent significant time as a participant in community service, then as a student leader organizing service experiences for my peers, as a community engagement professional, and eventually as a scholar of service-learning and community engagement. In each of these roles, I have been challenged to consider my own efficacy as a civic actor, to consider the value or consequence of the service performed to the communities with/for whom we worked, and to consider the curricular elements that would best support meaningful learning and development experiences for the participating students. I have always simultaneously juggled this sense that I was doing my best alongside a belief and expectation that I could be doing more and better.

Robert Rhoads (1997) spent six years following students in community service experiences and arrived at the concept of "critical community service." His recognition of work in communities as important spaces for student learning and development and his push to ensure that we interrogated these experiences in and with communities to consider questions of sustained inequality, privilege, and power were significant in shaping my thinking about what service-learning could and should be. Two of his principles for critical community service: that it is "intended to create social change, and therefore it is expected that participants engaged in the larger struggle to improve social conditions" and that this work is "part of the larger struggle to create a more liberatory form of education" heavily influenced my imaginings of what a critical service-learning pedagogy might be and do (p. 228). His research gave me space to question my own service experiences and to begin to think differently about the service-learning opportunities that I was involved in planning.

When I discovered Cynthia Rosenberger's (2000) description of critical service-learning, I was immediately compelled by her connection to Freirian pedagogy and its liberatory aims and her insistence that our efforts through service should go "beyond the work of taking care of immediate needs to community action that frees people from those needs" (p. 31). Born out of frustration at her experiences with engaged teaching, Rosenberger's conceptualization taught me to look critically at my own efforts at praxis. Her explicit call for equity and justice through service-learning was important reading for me, as a doctoral student, as it allowed me to believe that I could exercise such a commitment through my teaching. It was also inspiring as it expressed confidence in the possibility that service-learning could be critical and, in its criticality, truly work towards the change that felt suggested but not realized in the decades of service-learning that preceded Rhoads's and Rosenberger's contributions.

My work to operationalize critical service-learning was, in part, an effort to make sense of the literature in the field that challenged or questioned aspects of practice that reinscribed already unequal power asymmetries and did more harm than good in local communities. It was also an effort to articulate some specific tasks that felt needed and necessary for service-learning to actualize a commitment to social justice. If service-learning is (or could be), in Nadinne Cruz's (1994) definition, "a process of integrating intention with action in the context of movement toward a just relationship," then critical service-learning, as I outlined in 2008, enacts that process by bringing attention to social change, working to redistribute power, and developing authentic relationships.

These tasks have never felt simple and I have not endeavored to present them as a magic bullet for all community engaged work. The work to make service-learning critical is a process, an ongoing commitment, that must be made, affirmed, assessed and reassessed, deepened, strengthened, and made again. In my efforts to live into a critical service-learning pedagogy, I have encountered institutional barriers, financial barriers, actual physical barriers, and barriers of my own making (and thinking). And I have found partners and built relationships that have either helped me to eliminate those barriers or sustained me for the battles necessary to continue despite them. Critical service-learning, or the work involved to make service-learning critical, requires community building in our institutions and in the locations where we partner to leverage the support, to identify the work, to sustain the relationships that make change possible.

I am excited by Coffey and Arnold's effort to marry critical service-learning (Mitchell, 2008) and critical civic empathy (Mirra, 2018) as process and outcome of this work for a social-justice oriented community engagement praxis. Mirra (2018) sees critical civic empathy as "imaginatively embodying the lives of our fellow citizens while keeping in mind the social forces that differentiate our experiences as we make decisions about our shared public future" (p. 7). The idea, as prompted in this book, is that by utilizing critical service-learning—by being attentive to and bringing attention to social change, by working to redistribute power, and by developing authentic relationships in and through service—we develop the awareness in our students (and ourselves) that "we are individuals who constantly are negotiating our positions in society and need to deconstruct what we take for granted" in order to be wholly empathetic to the experiences of others (Mirra, 2018, p. 8). This awareness, then, "allows for the kind of connections that are needed to break through the forces of divisiveness and polarization that structure our civic life" (Mirra, p. 8). The critical service-learning opportunities we design should develop critical civic empathy in our students (which helps them get, as Coffey and Arnold aim for, "comfortable with the idea of being advocates for change"), and, ultimately, contribute to more just lives for the people in the communities where we serve.

The embrace of critical service-learning, as exemplified through the attempts and stumblings, commitments and practices, that Heather Coffey and Lucy Arnold so carefully outline in this text, feels important as a field leans into its desires and responsibility to work for a more just world. May this text inspire its readers with possibilities aligned with and extending beyond the resources offered in these pages so that we continue to advance and change our community engagement practice towards social justice.

## References

Cruz, N. (1994, November 11). Notes of the author: Reexamining service-learning in an international context [Workshop]. Annual Conference of the National Society for Experiential Education, Washington, D.C.

Mirra, N. (2018). *Educating for empathy: Literacy learning and civic engagement.* Teachers College Press.

Mitchell, T. D. (2008). Traditional vs. critical service-learning: Engaging the literature to differentiate two models. *Michigan Journal of Community Service Learning, 14*(2), 50–65.

Rhoads, R. A. (1997). *Community service and higher learning: Explorations of the caring self.* State University of New York Press.

Rosenberger, C. (2000). Beyond empathy: Developing critical consciousness through service learning. In C. R. O'Grady (Ed.), *Integrating service learning and multicultural education in colleges and universities* (pp. 23–43). Lawrence Erlbaum Associates.

Westheimer, J., & Kahne, J. (2004). What kind of citizen? The politics of educating for democracy. *American Educational Research Journal, 41*(2), 237–269.

# Preface

THIS BOOK WAS WRITTEN OUT of a need for critical service-learning faculty, students, and community partners to understand the actionable elements of critical service-learning in their classrooms and community spaces. The tools we offer in this book provide a thorough background on critical service-learning, a tool to use for shared reflection and analysis, and specific examples and ideas for implementation.

Some readers may find it most useful to read through this book in order, and we've arranged it to be friendly toward folx new to critical service-learning and even service-learning generally. That said, some readers may find that reading chapters in order of urgency and current needs may be more useful.

In Chapter 1, we lay out our argument for critical service-learning, specifically referencing some of the recent academic conversations on the topic. In Chapter 2, we provide a more detailed academic literature review and philosophical framework for faculty interested in making the case for critical service-learning in their own contexts.

In Chapters 3 and 4, we offer the Critical Service-Learning Implementation Model (CSLIM), a tool for implementing and reflecting on critical service-learning in classrooms and community spaces.

In Chapter 5, we delve into teaching strategies for critical service-learning faculty and discuss how to develop critical service-learning syllabi with an eye toward power dynamics and social justice. In Chapter 6, we continue to develop specific pedagogical tools by focusing on reflective cycles. In Chapter 7, we describe a detailed framework for faculty development, including a model for institutional support.

Chapter 8 offers some concluding thoughts with attention to online critical service-learning, the pandemic, and politics.

We are grateful to all of you reading this book and look forward to engaging in many joyful and challenging conversations with critical service-learning faculty, students, and community partners who are reading.

# ॐ Positioning Ourselves as Critical Service-Learning Faculty

O VER THE LAST TWO DECADES, we have engaged in a variety of critical pedagogies that facilitate social justice. Both former middle and secondary English language arts teachers turned higher education faculty, we have found value in critical service-learning as a pedagogy to challenge social injustice and to introduce our students to structural inequality. In what follows, we chronicle our experience with service-learning pedagogies and introduce a new tool for exploring the characteristics of *critical* service-learning (CSL) and its potential for building a curriculum to empower students in postsecondary settings.

## Heather's Story

Over the past 15 years, I have developed and taught service-learning courses for preservice teachers as preparation for diverse student populations. Using a variety of established models for service-learning (e.g., Investigate, Plan, Action, Reflect, Demonstrate [IPARD]; Preparation, Action, Reflection, and Celebration [PARC]; youth participatory action research), I carefully construct community-based experiences to challenge preservice teacher candidates to develop an understanding of how community and nonprofit organizations support the needs of underserved groups, especially in terms of public education. Throughout my experience with service-learning, first as a doctoral candidate and now as a professor in teacher preparation, I have transformed my research agenda and teaching to expose the importance of CSL in developing justice-oriented teachers.

My initial experience with service-learning was as a thinking partner for a friend who was developing a Children's Defense Fund (CDF) Freedom School on a historically Black college/university (HBCU) campus. Through this experience, I was exposed to the powerful benefits that culturally sustaining pedagogies (Paris & Alim, 2014) have on children of color, who are often marginalized by the traditional public school pedagogy and curriculum steeped in White supremacy. As a doctoral candidate, I taught introductory education courses in a Master of Arts in Teaching program at a large predominantly White institution (PWI), and I viewed this Freedom School as an opportunity to challenge the perspectives and counter the experiences of the mostly White, female preservice teachers in the program. For most of them, this experience placed them in the minority for the first time in their lives, which challenged their beliefs about how school might look if the roles were reversed (Moore et al., 2011). These future educators were able to observe and learn from African American Servant Leader Interns (SLIs) using culturally relevant pedagogy and curriculum they were trained to use at the Haley Farm in Clinton, Tennessee. As SLIs, these community members (often college students) develop a deep understanding of the importance of an Integrated Reading Curriculum (IRC) centered on multicultural literature representative of their summer scholars. They also began to understand the importance and value of empowering these young scholars through developing the development of their voice and agency, a foundational characteristic of the CDF Freedom Schools model. While teaching this summer Introduction to Education course with a service-learning experience shadowing SLIs and tutoring CDF scholars, I did not yet realize that there was a difference between traditional service-learning and CSL. In fact, at that point in 2006, CSL was not even a published framework.

Although we only dabbled in the interrogation of traditional schooling models in the first year of this field experience, we made changes in the second year that can be categorized as CSL. We brought the CDF Freedom Schools SLIs to the PWI campus to teach preservice teachers about their IRC and the role of multicultural literature. We also focused on the history of Black education in the United States and used our context of a PWI and an HBCU as a model for the diversity of educational experiences. This opportunity provided my introduction to CSL.

During this time, I also had the opportunity to teach an undergraduate service-learning course for preservice teachers as part of their scholarship enrichment program. Over the course of the fall semester, I learned how community and nonprofit organizations in the college town supported the needs of underrepresented residents. For example, students had the opportunity to work with a variety of organizations that supported the needs of displaced refugees from Myanmar, newly settled children of migrant farmworkers from

Central America, children with developmental disabilities, families of terminally ill children while they were receiving medical treatment, and local residents seeking to build bicycles from recycled parts. Teaching this course and researching the outcomes for preservice teachers (Coffey, 2010) provided me with a framework for engaging service participants in dialogue about perceptions and created a model for how assignments in future service-learning courses might be developed to prepare teachers for diverse classrooms.

These experiences set forth my path in teaching, research, and service as an assistant professor in the college of education at a large public university in the southeastern United States. Soon after beginning my career in higher education, I was asked to help in the development of a civic minor in urban youth and communities. This interdisciplinary program focuses on civic engagement and service-learning designed to prepare undergraduates to become informed and engaged citizens by providing them an opportunity to be agents of change in their community. I became an instructor of the foundational course in this program, which gave me the opportunity to continue to explore the potential of service-learning curriculum in teacher preparation. Through multiple research studies, I developed my own theories around preservice teachers, community partners, and middle-grades students.

Through teaching service-learning courses semester after semester, I developed a more critical lens regarding the inequities in society that cause a need for these community partners. As I began to more deeply understand the people we were serving in the university community, I also developed a pedagogy and curriculum that introduced my students to inequitable social and economic structures and challenged them to question these hierarchies as well. Teaching at a large, diverse university in one of the largest cities in the southeastern United States positioned me to engage my undergraduate students in a critique of the inequitable resource distribution in the communities and schools in which we were serving.

Most recently, as I develop more community partners that serve the needs of our high-poverty urban community members, I see the need to guide my students in a critical examination of the factors that hinder public school education and keep those living in poverty from upward mobility. I also seek opportunities for my students to work with community organizations that support the needs of public school students who are homeless or living in transition. Each semester, I also work with schools within the community so that my students can see firsthand how the work of these organizations directly impacts the students in the area schools. Throughout the 10 years that I have been teaching this course, I have endeavored to develop a more critical approach to service-learning, one that actually challenges my undergraduates (and myself) to interrogate the foundational causes of the needs for these community organizations. My practice has evolved into teaching more about social inequity and less about the actual activity associated with service-learning. In making this change, I have developed a list of behaviors that I've noticed among my own students as well as in the public school classrooms in which they tutor and mentor. This list and these observations are the foundation for the Critical Service-Learning Implementation Model or CSLIM.

## Lucy's Story

It's a trope of sorts that teachers want practical, hands-on activities, lesson plans, and ideas for the classroom, eschewing *theory*. Workshops, educational materials, and books for teachers often tout *ideas you can use—tomorrow!* Every choice we make in the classroom, however, stems from a philosophical stance; there is no atheoretical or apolitical teaching. Now, the reasons we enact certain practices may be that we are told to teach a certain thing or use a particular strategy; but then we are still enacting a theory. It just may be someone else's theory, or we may be enacting ideologies that don't match our goals as teachers. When we engage in praxis, our own theories influence our practice. I read Paulo Freire's (1970) *Pedagogy of the Oppressed* during my third year as a high school English teacher, and my understanding of critical literacy has influenced every move I've made in the classroom since. What I see as my work as a teacher educator, which began when I worked as a curriculum coordinator for a public school district and continues now that I teach future P–12 teachers in teacher preparation programs, is helping teachers understand the ways that theories connect to their classroom choices.

A story I share with my own students comes from a podcast episode called "How to Become Batman" produced by *Invisibilia* (Shaw & Natisse, 2015). In the episode, a psychologist describes studies done on rats and expectations and how the perception of the lab assistant holding the rat impacts the performance of that rat in a maze. This work suggests that very small actions, the way the rats are held and spoken to, make a difference. As teachers, the possibilities we imagine for our students and what potential we believe they have influence how we talk to them and how we treat them, even when we are performing scripted lessons. I firmly believe that the way we think about the world *matters*, and this way of thinking eventually set me on my journey with CSL.

My first years in the high school English classroom were spent teaching International Baccalaureate (IB) students; these students attended the school as a part of a magnet program. One of the required components of the IB diploma is community service, and it was through my participation in these service activities that I first began to understand the pitfalls of service-learning and praxis. On the one hand, it was easy for community service to become a sort of bureaucratic hoop for students and teachers to navigate. I saw a good amount of technical service happening, activities during which students traded their time for IB diplomas.

On the other hand, I participated in service-learning that cannot be termed critical but that certainly helped me understand the difference between charity orientations toward service-learning and change orientations (Kahne & Westheimer, 1996). One of the most popular service-learning projects was tutoring elementary school children in a high needs school; although the IB students almost always entered these tutoring relationships with a charity perspective, thinking they were "giving" help or knowledge to these children, many of them recognized by the end of the school year that they were forming mutually beneficial relationships with the children they were tutoring and would often notice that they were gaining value at least as much as they were offering to the children. Some of the IB students recognized the systemic oppression the children were experiencing and noticed the educational inequalities between their experiences and the children they were tutoring; these students were able to shift to a change orientation as a result of their experiences. Our program, however, was not critical, and support was not in place to help them develop greater critical consciousness or imagine possibilities for social change beyond their individual acts of tutoring.

This story demonstrates the impact of theory on practice. Although our program enacted a service-learning pedagogy, without critical theory, the move to social change was not possible. When teachers and students engage in service-learning with an orientation toward charity, the results of that service-learning activity are different than when teachers and students engage in service-learning with an orientation toward change. It is also important to realize that students are capable of making their own philosophical moves; students I worked with often did, even without programmatic support for those shifts. Without a critical pedagogy on the part of the teacher and program, however, these student shifts were more sporadic. More important, there are fewer opportunities for collaborative work toward social change.

When I began teaching college writing courses, I continued to include service-learning as a component of the course. One semester, I partnered with a fourth-grade teacher in our local school district. My college students completed similar activities (like dialogic journals) and even did some of the same readings as the fourth graders. Then, some of the college students went to the fourth-grade classroom to read and write with the elementary school students. Although I was not yet engaging in CSL specifically, my course did take a critical approach, and our class considered the social stratification that happens and asked questions about race, class, and gender made possible by their engagement with the elementary school community, including teachers, students, and parents. This work led me to research on CSL, which eventually became my dissertation.

By the time I wrote that dissertation, I had moved from university teaching to community college teaching and did my research on CSL in the context of a community college writing course. As we talk about in much greater detail in this book, my experience with CSL at the high school, university, and community college suggests many similarities in approach. There are some unique and important characteristics of community college work and students that researchers and theorists must keep in mind. I have found explorations of Ira Shor's (1980) work particularly helpful, as he has applied critical pedagogy in community college contexts.

Now, I teach and work in a new context for me: a small, minority-serving, liberal arts university. Over the past year, as I've learned about this new teaching context (amid a pandemic!), I've had new opportunities to explore what CSL might look like in the classroom. This year, I've had the opportunity to do CSL with dual-enrollment high school students and have worked on a prison outreach project, which provides a sharp look at the inequities of 2021 in the United States.

Although I originally set out to write this story as a "theory story," I now think that any such dichotomy between theory and my lived experience and work would be unproductive. Theory isn't something that happens when philosophers sit and ponder how and why things work; we enact theory; we live and play in theory when we choose to live consciously and reflectively. My identity as a queer woman, mom, and partner is as important as my early years teaching high school English and informs how I imagine systems of power, education, work, and social justice. Today, I'm reading Foucault's (1977) *Discipline and Punish* and Wilkerson's (2020) *Caste* as I prepare for CSL projects and coursework for the next semester and get ready to consider the connections between these texts, my own background and understandings, the connections and experiences of my students, and the connections and experiences of our community partners, who, right now, include prison activists and ministers. It's challenging work that is only going to become more challenging, and I am grateful for the energy of the folx who are willing to do this work with me, including my current and future CSL faculty peers.

## Our Mission

Using Heather's extensive experience with teaching service-learning courses and Lucy's deep theoretical understanding of the frameworks that support this work, we present this text as a guide for how other university instructors might implement a practice of CSL. In this text, we strive to share how we evolved in our understanding of how to approach this theory and method of teaching and how university administrators might support faculty in higher education to utilize this pedagogical approach to facilitate social justice and advocacy on their campuses.

As White middle-class cis-women, we occupy a privileged position within the space of higher education. If 2020 taught us anything, it is that the only way out is through; in this case, we must constantly confront and interrogate our privileges and our voices. Notions of White supremacy are a part of the dominant narrative of schooling in a myriad of ways, and it's not enough to declare an interest in or dedication to social justice in the big picture without a willingness to explore the nuanced biases and proclivities we've accumulated, often unconsciously. Developing a critical consciousness, a term often applied to class consciousness, is just as important to understanding how race plays a part in our lives and experiences. For us as White educators, we have to get comfortable with our discomfort (advice Lucy learned from *Star Trek*).

Reflecting uncomfortably is not easy or pleasant work, but it is joyful work and work we undertake because our students, our communities, and we ourselves are worth the effort. Developing skills for empathy and self-awareness benefit classrooms, universities, and our communities. In both this book and in the accompanying workbook, we offer our own reflective practices as CSL practitioners and suggest ways of grappling with the matrices of privilege.

## References

Coffey, H. (2010). *They* taught *me*: The benefits of early community-based field experiences in teacher education. *Teaching and Teacher Education, 26*(2), 335–342. https://doi.org/10.1016/j.tate.2009.09.014

Foucault, M. (1977). *Discipline and punish: The birth of the prison*. Pantheon Books.

Freire, P. (1970). *Pedagogy of the oppressed*. Seabury Press.

Kahne, J., & Westheimer, J. (1996, May). In the service of what? The politics of service learning. *The Phi Delta Kappan, 77*(9), 592–599. https://www.jstor.org/stable/20405655

Moore, K. T., Coffey, H., & Ewell, S. B. (2011). "Service is the rent we pay": A tale of how three teacher educators studied our own practice through engaging pre-service teachers in a multicultural service-learning experience. In T. Stewart & N. Webster (Eds.), *Exploring cultural dynamics and tensions within service-learning* (pp. 257–280). Information Age.

Paris, D., & Alim, H. S. (2014). What are we seeking to sustain through culturally sustaining pedagogy? A loving critique forward. *Harvard Educational Review, 84*(1), 85–100. https://doi.org/10.17763/haer.84.1.982l873k2ht16m77

Shaw, Y., & Natisse, K. M. (Hosts). (2015, January 23). How to become Batman [Audio podcast episode]. *Invisibilia*. https://www.npr.org/programs/invisibilia/378577902/how-to-become-batman

Shor, I. (1980). *Critical teaching & everyday life*. The University of Chicago Press.

Wilkerson, I. (2020). *Caste: The origins of our discontents*. Random House.

# ONE

#  The Case for Developing Social Justice Through Critical Service-Learning

ACCORDING TO BRAMELD (1965/2000), "EDUCATION has two major roles: to transmit culture and to modify culture. When American culture is in a state of crisis, the second of these roles–that of modifying and innovating–becomes more important" (p. 75). These words especially ring true as we write this text in 2021, which follows a year that challenged the world with a global pandemic and highlighted racial inequalities present in the United States. The backdrop of our current work occurs amid a global health crisis and after what arguably has been the most controversial election in the history of the United States. Educators across all age levels and content areas are experiencing a kind of exhaustion never before imagined due to the support they are providing for their traumatized students, participating in constant virtual meetings and online instruction, and navigating the many crises that have arisen due to the COVID-19 pandemic. Those educators committed to social justice have had to find new ways to support their students in virtual learning environments in an attempt to find equitable solutions for students living in a digital desert. Now, more than ever before, teachers in prekindergarten through Grade 16 must support students by promoting equity and helping students to understand the relationship between power and oppression (Matteson & Boyd, 2017). Although we write this in a time when participating in service-learning is mired in questions about safety and health issues, we argue that we must continue to strive to build capacity to meet the growing needs of communities by engaging in service-learning. By continuing to engage in critical service-learning (CSL), educators can create spaces where students can engage in social action to improve conditions for their communities.

In 2018, Nicole Mirra challenged English educators to prioritize the development of empathy in students as a major goal for the future of education. More specifically, she argued for a version of empathy that eschews a narrow focus on individual relationships in order to center empathy as "explicitly committed to grappling with inequities in our public life and engagement with democratic power structures" (Mirra, 2018, p. 7). She called this new concept "critical civic empathy" and posed the question of how we might think about individuals with differing perspectives from our own. Calling to mind Atticus Finch's claim, "You never really understand a person until you consider things from his point of view . . . until you climb inside of his skin and walk around in it" (Lee, 1960, p. 36), she called on educators to imagine what fellow citizens experience based on social and political forces.

As we write this text a year and a half into a global pandemic, we understand the urgent need to engender critical civic empathy. We are currently struggling with COVID-19, which has truly exposed the inequitable distribution of resources and power roles in society beyond our wildest imaginations. The pandemic revealed to the public these critical issues of inequity in American public schooling that we, as former teachers and current teacher educators for social justice, have been railing against for decades.

Thus, as we strive to support our college students as they develop critical civic empathy and prepare for their future careers in a variety of fields, we must focus on developing a deeper understanding of the fundamental causes of inequitable distribution of resources and its ties to racism, gender inequality, sexism, homophobia, and a host of other -isms that marginalize and oppress.

## What Is CSL?

In her seminal article for the *Michigan Journal of Community Service Learning*, Tania Mitchell (2008) defines CSL as a transformative pedagogy that moves participants "to see themselves as agents of social change, and use the experience of service to address and respond to injustice in communities" (p. 51). Contending that traditional service-learning focuses more on outcomes for the student, Mitchell (2008, p. 53) explains that CSL focuses on social change, working to redistribute power, and the development of authentic relationships. (See Figure 1.1 for Mitchell's visual representation of the difference between service-learning and CSL.) These elements are key to differentiating CSL because traditional service-learning can often resemble its critical counterpart. For example, examining diversity or "fixing" problems in communities are often elements of traditional service-learning (Mitchell, 2008, p. 57).

Conversely, CSL programs are interested in the power dynamics and social structures that underlie such problems and inequalities. For CSL programs, "serving" the community is not sufficient; CSL participants work alongside communities to be catalysts for social change. Later in this text, we provide examples of service-learning pedagogy and demonstrate how these practices might be reenvisioned to support a CSL pedagogy.

Often, we see CSL courses embedded in human services majors such as nursing, counseling, and teaching, in which working to dismantle preconceived notions is imperative and the concept of service itself is an accepted, if fraught, component of these traditionally feminized fields. Potentially, one of the most important sites of CSL work is in preservice teacher preparation programs in which the majority of future teachers are young, middle-class White women endeavoring to teach an increasingly diverse P–12 student population. To echo Boyd (2017, p. 10) on the need for social justice literacies, we don't need CSL in teacher education because so many teacher candidates are White; we need it because our teaching contexts are steeped in oppression. This need for positioning also comes in the health care field, in which the majority of undergraduates, like preservice teacher candidates, are White women who will serve the needs of patients who do not share a similar cultural background. Although it is necessary for practicing teachers to better understand the ways in which they are positioned and how they position students, our hope is that participating in CSL as an undergraduate will encourage future teachers, nurses, social workers, pediatricians, and others to continue the work of CSL and bring it to their future practice and their colleagues.

These fields are already doing CSL in many contexts, but many other majors and fields of study would also benefit from this kind of work. Fields such as computer science, math, history, economics, and science, among others, often have disciplinary divisions between theory and practice, and inequities in race, gender, class, sexual orientation, and ethnicity are certainly present, both in the fields themselves and in the problems explored in those fields. CSL offers opportunities for faculty in a variety of disciplines to attend to social justice and inequities in these fields as well.

Mirra's (2018) framework for critical civic empathy provides some defining principles for the work that we have attempted to do with CSL and offers a conduit through which to develop the kind of empathy that has the potential to bridge the gaps between what undergraduates assume about their communities and what they actually observe and reflect on in society. Mirra (2018) challenges us to (a) analyze the social position, power, and privilege of all people involved in the conversation; (b) focus on how personal experiences matter to each person and provide context for perspective; and (c) engage in "democratic dialogue and civic action committed to equity and justice (p. 7)." All these components are intended outcomes of our vision of CSL and provide us with a set of guidelines for evaluating our own practice.

CSL tends toward activities that promote social change and activism; reflection and self-awareness are key components (Mitchell, 2008). In attempting to develop some practical understanding of CSL as a discrete activity, Butin (2015) suggests some ways of assessing whether CSL has taken place, particularly critiquing too much alignment between service-learning activities the typical activities of a course, like grading, time progression in semesters, and centering of teachers over community partners.

## The Growing Popularity of Service-Learning

Internationally, institutions of higher education have been using service-learning pedagogy to introduce university students to the idea of civic empathy for more than 50 years. Although not always focused on a more critical application of service-learning, universities around the world often engage undergraduates in service that manifests in the form of volunteerism, tutoring, charity work, and long-term study abroad and spring-break trips.

Service-learning, while already widely implemented on university campuses, is becoming more popular on many 2-year college campuses as well. After all, community colleges attract a wide swath of students, from displaced workers hoping to gain a new certification or skill set to students hoping to complete general education requirements and transfer to a 4-year school. To frame this discussion in numbers, according to the College Board, 7.2 million undergraduate students were enrolled as either full- or part-time students at 2-year institutions in 2014 (Ma & Baum, 2016, p. 2). These 7.2 million students made up about a quarter of U.S. undergraduates in 2014; students at public 4-year colleges, private 4-year colleges, and for-profit colleges make up the other 75% (Ma & Baum, 2016, p. 3). Furthermore, as the College Board documents, 2-year schools serve a significant proportion of students of color, low-socioeconomic-status students, and first-generation college students. The College Board calculates that Black and Hispanic students each compose 29% of the total undergraduate population at public 4-year colleges, while Black students compose 44% and Hispanic students comprise 56% of students at 2-year colleges (Ma & Baum, 2016, p. 6).

## Why CSL Anyway?

In "To Hell with Good Intentions," a 1968 speech to American volunteers, Austrian philosopher Ivan Illich (1968/1990) criticizes the idea of international service and directly questions how we can send "well-meaning" university students to do charity work around the world without adequate preparation. He challenges university faculty and students to think deeply about how these service providers are not aware of the communities, cultures, and languages in which they will be immersed and that both the service providers and, especially, the recipients are harmed by this under preparation. Although these service providers intend to "do good," they often enter the experience thinking how they might fix or save the world, thus encouraging them to participate without critical reflection and to walk away from the experience with a deficit perspective of the community they helped. Essentially, these service providers are engaging in traditional service-learning—the kind that dips them into the experience but does not challenge them to examine the systemic social issue at play that necessitates the service.

Mitchell (2008) differentiates CSL as service-learning projects with explicit social justice orientations, which suggests that students must address issues of institutional inequality. Butin (2015), however, problematizes the actual impact of CSL: "This distinction—that desires are just that, desires—offers one the space to step back and to better understand what one's dreams of justice have accomplished" (p. 7). For Butin (2015), considering the actual effects of service-learning is an important part of the process, and he makes a case for some specific metrics to determine whether service-learning is critical or not; such metrics include whether the service-learning coincides with the timeline of the course, whether a final paper is the primary source of assessment, and the degree of engagement between the teacher and the community partners (pp. 8–9). These are practical metrics that Butin phrases as questions, but his prior point about the *desire* for social justice is also worth considering from a critical perspective. Butin seems to suggest that even a desire for social justice is a product of the capitalist institutions within which CSL pedagogies operate. His response to those desires, these dreams, is to interrupt them, to "suggest that educators may need to wake up to the pedestrian realities around them and embrace such real-world dreams to begin to truly dream again" (Butin, 2015, p. 9).

While acknowledging how empowering CSL has been for researchers and teachers in higher education, Butin (2015) suggests that it may not be accomplishing its actual aims of reciprocity and collaboration between institutions and community partners and the movement toward social transformation. His questions are important to parse because the research on CSL is snared in its own enculturation into higher education. Researchers who study CSL (like us) are universally members of academia and do not represent community partners. Because there are rarely benefits to publication for most such community partners, benefits of research and publication fall primarily to higher education faculty and graduate students.

Lewis et al. (2007) describe this problem of research (although not specifically on the topic of CSL); they examine the relationships between researchers and K–12 teachers and students and argue that the reorientation of the relationships between them is a crucial component of liberatory research. They argue, "Rather than merely consuming knowledge, participants who collaborate with researchers engage in the production of knowledge" (Lewis et al., 2007, p. 4). Thus, although participants may not benefit from publication in the same ways that university researchers do, it is important to include them in the process of creating knowledge about K–12 classrooms. Lewis et al.'s thinking applies to CSL; as college faculty, we must think carefully about reciprocity, but there are a number of ways to do this work. Rather than college faculty like us or Butin (2015) determining whether CSL is happening, including community stakeholders in conversations about whether the aims of critical service-learning are being achieved is critical.

Research conducted and reported by university faculty and students can easily take on that paternalistic attitude toward community partners and participants; community partners can become the "objects" of CSL, at least in the documentation of the process, when their voices are not included. Freire (1998), in describing critical learning, notes that "learners will be engaged in a continuous transformation through which they become authentic subjects of the construction and reconstruction of what is being taught, side by side with the teacher, who is equally subject to the same process" (p. 33). If critical learning and teaching represent the democratizing stance between teachers and students, it makes sense that critical research on CSL should have a similar democratizing force. All of this is not to say that Butin (2015) does not have a point; he very well may, and, ultimately, the portrayal of CSL in the literature of the field is important, especially to how it continues to be constructed and carried out.

What we as CSL faculty need is a way to track and include the voices of our students and community partners in our assessment and understanding of CSL. In Chapter 3, Heather provides some additional personal context for the development of the CSLIM, but providing a framework for community partners and students to make sense of this pedagogy is part of our motivation in developing this model as well.

## The CSLIM

CSLIM was originally developed as a means by which to identify the observational behaviors and characteristics of K–12 teachers who engaged in CSL. Over the course of a 3-year study of working with middle school teachers who annually involve their eighth-grade students in The Responsible Change Project (Coffey & Fulton, 2018), a pattern of certain repetitive, specific practices identified by Mitchell (2008) began to emerge. Some of those practices included

- "drawing attention to root causes of social problems, and involving students in actions and initiatives addressing root causes" (Mitchell, 2008, p. 51).
- "encourag[ing] students to see themselves as agents of social change, and use the experience of service to address and respond to injustice in communities" (Mitchell, 2008, p. 51).

Drawing on the existing research in the field related to teacher practices in (K–12) classrooms that engaged in CSL and observations of teachers participating in a related research study, CSLIM was developed directly from noticings from classroom instruction and student engagement with the curriculum. Presented in more detail in Chapter 3, the four major categories that emerged from 3 years of observation of two classrooms included (1) pedagogy (teacher decision-making and practices), (2) observable student behaviors (i.e., interactions and practices), (3) space (classroom layout and dynamics), and (4) curriculum (standards, activities, and lessons). Developed while Heather was collecting data for another research project related to her role as the director of the National Writing Project site at the university where she teaches, CSLIM presents specific behaviors and actions evident in CSL experiences. We present a fully developed (and malleable) model that includes a description of these behaviors, which can be used by college faculty and administrators to develop a deeper understanding of how service-learning courses might be more heavily influenced by a charity or change orientation.

We argue for a social change approach to service-learning in order that students entering the workforce have a more nuanced understanding of the factors that limit the attainment of a socially just society. In what follows, we present literature to support the need for CSL, especially in preparation for careers that support the needs of the public; we propose a tool for preparation of course activities and discussions that facilitate this orientation; and we provide tacit examples from our own practice to support our argument. As college professors, we see our purpose to effectively prepare our students to engage in society beyond the walls of academia. Through their participation in CSL experiences, we want students to develop a deeper understanding of how rules and habits established long before our time prevent certain groups in society from climbing out of an intentional hole crafted by oppression and marginalization. At the very least, our goal is to teach students to uncover the foundational causes of inequality, and ideally, we hope they will develop critical civic empathy as they seek to work within the community to change oppressive structures.

## References

Brameld, T. (2000). *Education as power.* Caddo Gap Press. (Original work published 1965)

Boyd, A. (2017). *Social justice literacies in the English classroom: Teaching practice in action.* Teachers College Press.

Butin, D. (2015). Dreaming of justice: Critical service-learning and the need to wake up. *Theory into Practice, 54*(1), 5–10. https://doi.org/10.1080/00405841.2015.977646

Coffey, H., & Fulton, S. (2018). The Responsible Change Project: Building a justice-oriented middle school curriculum through critical service-learning. *Middle School Journal, 49*(5), 16–25. https://doi.org/10.1080/00940771.2018.1509560

Freire. P. (1998). *Pedagogy of freedom: Ethics, democracy, and civic courage.* Rowman & Littlefield.

Illich, I. (1990). To hell with good intentions. In J. C. Kendall (Ed.), *Combining service and learning: A resource book for community and public service* (Vol. 1, pp. 314–320). National Society for Internships and Experiential Education. (Original work published 1968)

Lee, H. (1960). *To kill a mockingbird.* Harper Collins.

Lewis, C., Enciso, P., & Moje, E. B. (2007). *Reframing sociocultural research on literacy: Identity, agency, and power.* Erlbaum.

Ma, J., & Baum, S. (2016, April). *Trends in community colleges: Enrollment, prices, student debt, and completion* (College Board Research Brief). College Board. https://trends.collegeboard.org/sites/default/files/trends-in-community-colleges-research-brief.pdf

Matteson, H., & Boyd, A. (2017). Are we making PROGRESS? A critical literacies framework to engage pre-service teachers for social justice. *Journal of Language and Literacy Education, 13*(1), 28–54. https://files.eric.ed.gov/fulltext/EJ1141489.pdf

Mirra, N. (2018). *Educating for empathy: Literacy learning and civic engagement.* Teachers College Press.

Mitchell, T. D. (2008, Spring). Traditional vs. critical service-learning: Engaging the literature to differentiate two models. *Michigan Journal of Community Service-Learning, 14*(2), 50–65. http://hdl.handle.net/2027/spo.3239521.0014.205

# TWO

# ∾ The Pedagogy of Critical Service-Learning

T HE PHRASE SERVICE-LEARNING WAS INITIALLY used in 1969 by the
Southern Regional Education Board (O'Grady & Chappell, 2000), who
defines service-learning as "the accomplishment of tasks that meet genuine
human needs in combination with conscious educational growth" (Stanton
et al., 1999). Jeff Claus and Curtis Ogden (1999) describe service-learning
as "the idea of engaging youth in educationally framed community service
activity" (p. 1). While Anderson (1998) presents a series of policy propos-
als to encourage service-learning in K–12 schools and higher education, this
position paper also provided a rationale for engaging in service-learning in
schools, including civic engagement and character development, a sense of
belonging for students, community building, and social justice (pp. 3–6).
Regardless of how it is defined, service-learning is a pedagogical strategy used
in K–16 educational settings. Although there are a variety of purposes for
service-learning, all iterations of the practice involve students participating in
community service and reflection on service as a part of coursework. Often,
these community service activities occur on campus where the course is being taught, at other educational institutions, or at a variety of other community locations, including churches, shelters, clinics, and community centers.

Although idealized as often mutually beneficial for participants and community partners, critics of service-learning point out that a majority of lead-
ing theorists in the field of service-learning are White, and the literature
rarely specifically interrogates issues of power, racism, oppression, or social
injustice (O'Grady & Chappell, 2000, p. 14). Meanwhile, the foundation of
*critical* service-learning (CSL) includes activities and readings that promote
social change and activism with reflection and self-awareness at the core of
CSL (Mitchell, 2008).

## Differentiating CSL From Traditional Service-Learning

Emerging from their analysis of service-learning projects in K–12 contexts,
Kahne and Westheimer (1996) delineate two orientations for service-learning:

charity and change. Educators with a charity orientation tend to focus on concepts like altruism and moral development in service-learning projects. Educators with a change orientation tend to focus on activism and transformation. This dichotomy is further taxonomized by Butin (2015), attempting to develop some practical understanding of critical service-learning as a distinct activity. Eschewing the charity/change dichotomy, Butin instead draws distinctions between technical, cultural, political, and anti-foundational service-learning. The *technical* perspective views service-learning as an educational best practice that engages students and connects them to course content (Butin, 2010, p. 8). The *cultural* perspective organizes service-learning as a way to improve democracy and allow people to connect with various and diverse perspectives (Butin, 2010, pp. 9–10). The *political* perspective is concerned with power imbalances and access to power and legitimacy (Butin, 2010, p. 11). Whereas the *antifoundational* perspective encourages the breaking down of binaries and certainties, approaching knowledge from, as Butin (2010) puts it, "a position of doubt rather than certainty" (pp. 13–14). These later two perspectives stem from philosophical traditions, with critical theory, which Butin (2015) calls political, on one hand, and poststructural or postmodern, which Butin terms antifoundational.

Butin (2015) also suggests that alignment between service-learning experiences and the typical activities of a course, such as grading, time progression in semesters, and centering teachers over community partners, renders the critical almost impossible; he argues that many practices considered CSL actually are not and includes a list of bullet points that clarifies the practice of CSL that make the work an actual implemented practice and not a "dream" or a "theory." On the other hand, practices without a thoughtful ideological perspective also are not CSL (Steele, 2021).

CSL as defined by Mitchell (2008) is situated somewhere on a spectrum between the cultural, political, and antifoundational perspectives of service-learning, and examining how these perspectives are entwined and how they are not is useful. It is also useful to note that critical service-learning, although a subset of service-learning, may also contain many variations and subcategories. See Figure 2.1 for the distinctions among the cultural, political, and antifoundational perspectives of service-learning.

When teachers and students engage in service-learning with an orientation toward charity, the results of that service-learning activity are different from when teachers and students are engaging in service-learning with an orientation toward change. It is also important to realize that students are capable of making their own philosophical moves, even without programmatic support for those shifts. Without a critical pedagogy on the part of the teacher and program, however, these student shifts will be more sporadic. More important, there are fewer opportunities for collaborative work toward social change—cultural, political, and anti-foundational.

*Focus on Social Injustice*

In noting the similarities between traditional service-learning and CSL, Mitchell (2008) argues that cycles of reflection and connections between classroom learning and work in the community are components of both types of service-learning. There are significant differences in the core of the work, however, with traditional service-learning focusing on "serving to learn" and "learning to serve" (Mitchell, 2008, p. 53); she contends that traditional service-learning focuses more on outcomes for the student (Mitchell, 2008, p. 52). On the other hand, CSL focuses on acting for social change, working to redistribute power, and developing authentic relationships (Mitchell, 2008). See Figure 2.2 for Mitchell's visual representation of the difference between service-learning and critical service-learning.

## Theoretical Context for CSL

We draw on critical social theory to build out our argument related to ways that critical service-learning might impede the reproduction of inequality and justice in school settings. Critical social theorists (i.e., those from the Frankfurt school) and critical pedagogues concerned with oppressive and unjust relationships produced in traditional pedagogy challenge the model of the teacher at the front of the classroom transmitting knowledge.

This differentiation between traditional pedagogy and critical pedagogy can be particularly challenging in U.S. schools, as some of the drama unfolding at local school board meetings in 2021 makes evident. Mike Rose (2014) describes the way many people in the United States apply an understanding of individual motivation and goal setting to larger social inequities. Rose (2014) suggests the "pull yourself up by your bootstraps" (p. 10) model as

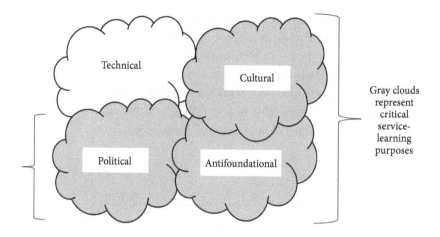

**Figure 2.1.** Differentiating Critical Service-Learning.

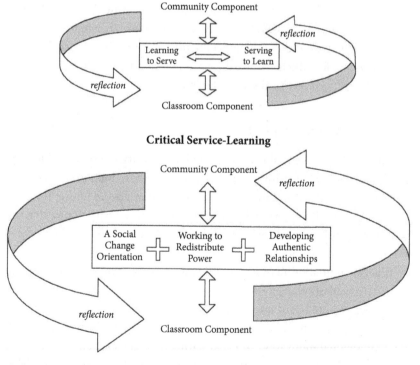

**Figure 2.2.** Traditional vs. Critical Service-Learning (Mitchell, 2008, p. 53.)

one that ascribes success to an individual's (or family's) determination. Many traditional service-learning programs stem from a similar philosophy of "helping" people who may have had a bad situation or have made mistakes. CSL perspectives, however, incorporate the broader understanding of social structures that Rose (2014) describes while trying to maintain some grasp on individual motivation:

> It does not diminish the importance of individual commitment and effort also to acknowledge the tremendous role played in achievement by the kind, distribution, and accessibility of institutions, programs, and other resources. And these resources, as everybody knows, are not equally available. (pp. 10–11)

The focus on social injustice by CSL proponents indicates this understanding of the way people are impacted by social structures, institutions, and history.

## CSL and Subject/Object Relationships

People impacted by social forces are actual humans in the world of CSL; determining what problems "deserve" time and attention and who makes that decision are constant questions for participants, faculty, administrators, and community partners. How this question is resolved varies from context to context, but all too often, those "served" by service-learning students are the objects of the service and the learning instead of the empowered decision-makers with agency. These questions are further complicated by issues of race, class, and gender. Studies analyzing the participation of White preservice teachers in service-learning projects often focus on the learning that happens with the White teachers, whether the projects are viewed as successes or failures (Dooley & Burant, 2015; Jones et al., 2005; Ogden, 1999). There is limited work on service-learning projects completed by students of color, however. Butler et al. (2018) describe a CSL activity completed at a four-year university and found a significant impact on students of color and male students, which suggests that CSL may be particularly important for marginalized students. Similarly, Reed and Butler (2015) suggest that CSL can help marginalized students understand systemic inequities through a critical lens that they may then be able to apply to their own perspectives.

Seider et. al (2013), however, writing about the Social Action Program, a service-learning program initiated at a 4-year institution, describe students of color as less engaged in community building compared to their White peers as a result of the service-learning experiences. The researchers found that some of the reasons students of color felt less engaged in the activities had to do with their relationships with White students:

> Several of the students of color who participated in the current study also characterized their reluctance as due to concerns about appearing overly sensitive about issues of racism, as well as frustration with conveying their perspectives on race and racism to their White classmates. (Seider et al., 2013, p. 23)

Furthermore, even though the White students did experience more engagement with the project and more movement toward the social justice mindsets encouraged by the program, they still othered community members in their language choices:

> The language with which many White students in the Social Action Program discussed the individuals they encountered at their service placements revealed the extent to which they—either consciously or unconsciously—perceived these individuals to be a different "type" of person from themselves and their peers. (Seider et al., 2013, p. 24)

Seider et al.'s (2013) study, a mixed-methods analysis that combined statistical analysis of survey responses with a qualitative analysis of interviews with service-learning participants, suggests that students of color who participate in service-learning, at least alongside their White peers, may not benefit from the experiences in the same way that White students seem to because of their experience with the emotional labor around issues of race and racism.

To prepare students for CSL, the classroom needs to encourage students to develop an awareness of their own assumptions about race, class, gender, and social institutions. Boyle-Baise (2002) suggests that students should be provided a "framework to question the 'rightness' of one's views" (p. 17). Such frameworks include analysis of how different groups might think about and value ideas differently. Boyle-Baise (2002, p. 25) also points to the need for explicit discussion of justice, inclusion, antiracism, and other aims of service-learning geared toward social change. In one example of a tacit strategy for encouraging community among her students and moving toward the aims of service-learning for social change, Boyle-Baise (2002, p. 26) provides classroom opportunities for students to work in mixed-race groups with co-operative goals.

Another important move for CSL is the way community partners are received in the classroom by students and teachers. Social change is only possible when these relationships are "equal, reciprocal, and mutually beneficial" (Boyle-Baise, 2002, p. 17). The planning of CSL must then include community partnerships at every stage of the endeavor, including planning and classroom experiences. Boyle-Baise (2002, pp. 84–85) shares the power of her role as a university professor conducting service-learning activities with community partners by inviting them to be co-constructors and evaluators of the curriculum and student performance.

## Engendering CSL Through Writing and Reflection

Mitchell (2008) explains how CSL programs embed a social justice mindset, not only in community-focused work but also in the classroom:

> Service, itself, is a concept steeped in issues of identity and privilege which must be wrestled with for students to be effective in their service work. A critical service-learning program is intentional in its social change orientation and in its aim toward a more just and caring society; part of that intentionality is demonstrated in the concepts with which students engage in classroom discussions, readings, and writing assignments. (p. 55)

In CSL-oriented classrooms, such writing assignments prepare students to engage in service-learning by developing the habit of reflection and helping students develop a theoretical framework for engaging in service.

This critical perspective on reflection comes from the tradition of critical theory and transformational education; the process of reflection is a part of the development of critical consciousness. For the field of education, Freire's (1970) work in critical pedagogy and critical literacies also encourages the use of reflection for transformational education. As a counterperspective to Freire's anticapitalist pedagogy of hope, Seitz's (2020) pedagogy of disappointment creates space for students to resist the neoliberal version of hope: the happy worker.

Drawing from Freire's (1970) practice of problem posing, developing a classroom culture of inquiry is key to critical service-learning for Wilhelm et al. (2014), as they discuss the ways in which writing assignments develop that kind of a classroom culture: "prereading and prewriting activities that motivate and engage the students, that activate what they already care about and know, and then build upon this to prepare them" (p. 26). In this model of CSL, writing can engage students and value their prior knowledge. However, encouraging reflective cycles takes another step, as Wilhelm et al. (2014) also note: "Frontloading . . . uncovers assumptions and misconceptions that students may have about a topic that are important to articulate because this foregrounding makes these misconceptions imminently more susceptible to correction and accommodation" (p. 27). Writing assignments that prepare students for CSL also prepare them for self-analysis and self-awareness.

Other researchers argue that writing assignments move students from being critical consumers to critical creators of media. Lewis and Causey (2015) describe a series of class assignments that encourage students to critically interpret texts and then recontextualize those texts for their own purposes. The goals of these class activities are social justice and advocacy for issues that matter to the students (Lewis & Causey, 2015, p. 129). Johnson and Winn (2015) similarly argue for a literacy continuum that situates student writing and learning in a spectrum that includes social justice and advocacy.

In Chapter 6, we provide pragmatic approaches to implementing critical reflection in CSL courses.

## Critical Pedagogy as a Foundation for CSL

Freire (1998) argues that the "educator's task is to encourage human agency" (p. 10). Indeed, Freire (1998, pp. 69–70) argues that teachers must respect the autonomy of their students, even though the values of people are different. Furthermore, Freire (1998) rejects an acceptance of the system and argues for the possibility of agency as the very premise of education: "Educational practice itself, as an experience in humanization, must be impregnated with this ideal" (p. 103). For Freire, teaching is inextricable from believing in the possibility of agency for students and for humans.

The ways in which critical pedagogy is applied to CSL projects depend on both the institutional space available for service-learning and the participants themselves. For example, Stenhouse and Jarrett (2012) conducted a study on preservice teachers participating in a critical pedagogy version of service-learning; in this study, 66% of participants were White. The authors analyzed a service-learning project built on Shor's (1980) critical pedagogy principles, but in this study, that use of critical pedagogy applied to the preservice teachers, who were mostly White and female.

Additionally, Sprague Martinez et al. (2017) describe a critical service project conducted with youth of color as a part of a community-based learning activity. This project used an inquiry-based curriculum based on Freire's critical pedagogy and trained young teachers of color to facilitate the project with the young people (Sprague Martinez et al., 2017, pp. 72–73). This 10-week program was offered at an after-school program at a middle school in Boston, and the focus of the curriculum was health equity (Sprague Martinez et al., 2017, p. 72). Students in the program met with local health care workers and learned about the state of access to health care in their community; they then created educational materials for dissemination based on their research (Sprague Martinez et al., 2017, p. 77). In a survey conducted both pre- and post-activity, and despite mixed results on the surveys, researchers concluded that CSL provided participants with ways to resist unhealthy behaviors that were a part of their communities (Sprague Martinez et al., 2017, p. 85). These survey results suggest the existence of at least some possibilities for the impact of CSL on students of color, but there is room for more research, especially qualitative research, to understand the narratives engaged in by these students.

Reed and Butler (2015) describe CSL conducted by students at an urban middle school, where Reed, the public school teacher, had previously doubted the possibilities of critical service-learning with her students because they were so often the recipients of service. They argue that encouraging urban students to participate in CSL disrupts some of the stereotypes that others believe and that some of them have internalized. Reed and Butler (2015) suggest that "there are ways to effectively address social inequities in this country without pointing the finger of blame and shame at students whose families have some financial hardships" (p. 61); they contend that CSL allows students to develop an awareness of the social conditions that have led to their oppression, instead of accepting a normed responsibility for that condition.

In Green's (2001) reflections on a service-learning project that involved her majority White students tutoring at a majority Black school, she writes about the challenges that White students often face when doing service-learning projects and facing the realities of racial inequity. Her conclusion about the success of the service-learning project and the way her students construed race is instructive:

> The presence of students of color in the classroom made discussions of race harder for majority students to dismiss, and the ability of white and African American students to talk with one another across racial lines was, in my experience, exceptional. (Green, 2001, pp. 24–25)

This analysis centers the experiences of the White students and does not mention the challenges faced by students of color who were the objects of that transformation of the White students. Green goes on to talk about the importance of including students of color in the service-learning project, but there is little admission of the costs borne by those students of color, costs that are suggested in Seider et al.'s (2013) study that compared the experiences of White students and students of color involved in service-learning projects.

In this chapter, we have discussed the definition of CSL and a variety of ways in which the work is categorized. We also described connections to both reflection and agency and offered critiques of CSL. These understandings of how CSL is defined have also allowed us to demonstrate some of the critical needs in the field.

## Conclusion

Both research and the practical application of CSL have tremendous benefits for faculty and students in higher education; however, the appropriate implementation of strategies and behaviors in addition to the overwhelming amount of work discourages institutional implementation. We truly believe that CSL, if done well, not only has the potential to encourage critical analysis of structural inequalities among service providers but also has the power to mobilize community members who are positioned to advocate for their best interests. We leverage our extensive experience teaching service-learning courses and the development of mutually beneficial relationships with our community partners to develop CSLIM, a much-needed model for exploring the differences between service-learning and CSL.

# References

Anderson, S. (1998, September). *Service learning: A national strategy for youth development.* The Communitarian Network. https://citeseerx.ist.psu.edu/viewdoc/download?doi=10.1.1.955.9065&rep=rep1&type=pdf

Boyle-Baise, M. (2002). *Multicultural service learning: educating teachers in diverse communities.* Teachers College Press.

Butin, D. (2010). *Service-learning in theory and practice: The future of community engagement in higher education.* Palgrave MacMillan.

Butin, D. (2015). Dreaming of justice: Critical service-learning and the need to wake up. *Theory into Practice, 54*(1), 5-10. doi:10.1080/00405841.2015.977646

Butler, B. R., Coffey, H., & Young., J. L. (2018). Justice-oriented teaching dispositions in urban education: A critical interpretive case study. *Urban Education, 56*(2), 193–227. https://doi.org/10.1177/0042085918801428

Claus, J., & Ogden, O. (1999). *Service learning for youth empowerment and social change.* Peter Lang.

Dooley, J. C., & Burant, T. J. (2015). Lessons from preservice teachers: Under the surface of service-learning in teacher education. In O. Delano-Oriaran, M. W. Penick-Parks, & S. Fondrie (Eds.), *The SAGE sourcebook of service-learning and civic engagement* (pp. 325–332). SAGE Reference.

Freire, P. (1970). *Pedagogy of the oppressed.* Seabury Press.

Freire. P. (1998). *Pedagogy of freedom: Ethics, democracy, and civic courage.* Rowman & Littlefield.

Green, A. (2001, Fall). "But you aren't White:" Racial perceptions and service-learning. *Michigan Journal of Community Service-Learning, 8*, 18–26. http://hdl.handle.net/2027/spo.3239521.0008.102

Johnson, L. P., & Winn, M. T. (2015). Toward a literacy continuum. In E. Morrell & L. Scherff (Eds.), *New directions in teaching English: Reimagining teaching, teacher education, and research.* (pp. 49–58). Rowman & Littlefield.

Jones, S., Gilbride-Brown, J., & Gasiorski, A. (2005). Getting inside the "underside" of service-learning: Student resistance and possibilities. In D. W. Butin (Ed.), *Service-learning in higher education* (pp. 3–24). Palgrave.

Kahne, J., & Westheimer, J. (1996, May). In the service of what? The politics of service learning. *The Phi Delta Kappan, 77*(9), 592–599. https://files.eric.ed.gov/fulltext/ED375521.pdf

Lewis, C., & Causey, L. (2015). Critical engagement through digital media production. In E. Morrell & L. Scherff (Eds.), *New directions in teaching English: Reimagining teaching, teacher education, and research* (pp. 123–141). Rowman & Littlefield.

Mitchell, T. D. (2008, Spring). Traditional vs. critical service-learning: Engaging the literature to differentiate two models. *Michigan Journal of Community Service-Learning, 14*(2), 50–65. http://hdl.handle.net/2027/spo.3239521.0014.205

Ogden, C. (1999). Going beyond service. In J. Claus & C. Ogden (Eds.), *Service learning for youth empowerment and social change* (pp. 187–194). Peter Lang.

O'Grady, C. R., & Chapell, B. (2000). With, not for: the politics of service learning in multicultural communities. In C. J. Ovando & P. McLaren (Eds.), *The politics of multiculturalism and bilingual education: students and teachers caught in the crossfire* (pp. 209–224). McGraw Hill.

Reed, P., & Butler, T. (2015). Flipping the script: When service-learning recipients become service-learning givers. *Theory into Practice, 54*(1), 55–62. https://doi.org/10.1080/00405841.2015.977663

Rose, M. (2014). *Why school? Reclaiming education for all of us.* The New Press.

Seider, S., Huguley, J. P., & Novick, S. (2013, March). College students, diversity, community service learning. *Teachers College Record, 115*(3), 1–44. http://www.tcrecord.org.eu1.proxy.openathens.net/library/content.asp?contentid=16880

Seitz, D. K. (2020). "It's Not About You": Disappointment as queer pedagogy in community-engaged service-learning. *Journal of Homosexuality, 67*(3) 305–314, doi: 10.1080/00918369.2018.1528078.

Shor, I. (1980). *Critical teaching & everyday life.* The University of Chicago Press.

Sprague Martinez, L. S., Reich, A. J., Flores, C. A., Ndulue, U. J., Brugge, D., Gute, D. M., & Perea, F. C. (2017). Critical discourse, applied inquiry and public health action with urban middle school students: Lessons learned engaging youth in critical service-learning. *Journal of Community Practice, 25*(1), 68–89. https://doi.org/10.1080/10705422.2016.1269251

Stanton, T. K., Giles, D. E., & Cruz, N. I. (1999). *Service-learning: A movement's pioneers reflect on its origins, practice, and future.* Jossey-Bass.

Steele, L. (2021). *Dreams, theories, and pleasure: Providing an ideological backing for critical service-learning* [Paper presentation]. AERA 2021 Annual Conference. (Virtual).

Stenhouse, V. L., & Jarrett, O. S. (2012, Winter). In the service of learning and activism: Service learning, critical pedagogy, and the problem solution project. *Teacher Education Quarterly, 39*(1), 51–76. https://files.eric.ed.gov/fulltext/EJ977356.pdf

Wilhelm, J. D., Douglas, W., & Fry, S. W. (2014). *The activist learner: Inquiry, literacy, and service to make learning matter.* Teachers College Press.

# THREE

#  The Critical Service-Learning Implementation Model

IN THIS CHAPTER, WE PROVIDE the personal and theoretical support for the Critical Service-Learning Implementation Model (CSLIM) and offer a basic overview of the tool.

## Heather's Experience

When I first began teaching at the University of North Carolina at Charlotte, I wanted to incorporate service-learning into my courses. In my second year, I was asked to teach a liberal studies course, Service-Learning for Educators, and began the arduous process of seeking community partners. A native of the city in which my campus is located, I knew that the school system was large and had multiple areas of need. Within my first 3 years teaching the course, I had established partnerships with five (K–12) public schools and three community organizations. Although some of those partnerships were short-lived because of changing administrations and programming goals, one partnership with a local high school was impactful for both the undergraduates in the course and for the high school students with whom we were working.

The majority of my students were preservice teacher education majors, minoring in Urban Youth and Communities. The course provided the foundation for understanding the roles that nonprofit and community organizations play in supporting the underserved needs of schools. Through course readings and activities, students learned about the goals of service-learning, educational funding, the history of the large urban local school district, and a basic introduction to the idea of social justice. As the semester progressed, we met with community partners, who gave us deeper insight into the mission and goals of their organizations and their expectations for our participation. One of these partnerships was developed with a large urban high school, where one of my former students taught Advanced Placement (AP) Biology. She invited us to come get to know her students, who described their major project for the semester—a hydroponic greenhouse renovation.

Over the course of one semester, these mostly pre-service teachers worked with AP Biology students to clean out an abandoned greenhouse on the school campus while also learning about the role of hydroponic gardening. The high school students explained that they were developing a hydroponic greenhouse to teach the community about the potential of urban gardening to offset the negative outcomes from living in a food desert. So, as my students were engaging in a service-learning project with high school students, the high school students were participating in service-learning as well. During their conversations with the high school students, undergraduates realized that many of the high school students did not have formalized plans to attend college but had identified where they might go based on knowing someone who attended a college or university, mostly within the state. The undergraduates recognized the inherent problem with selecting a college based on knowing someone who went there and were concerned that these students would waste time and money attending institutions of higher education that might not have a major related to their interests. Thus, these undergraduates created a resource highlighting the academic majors and requirements for admittance into all the public universities in the state. Upon discussions with the guidance counselor, the participating teacher, and the assistant principal, the undergraduates learned that because the school had such a large population and guidance counselors had primarily been reallocated to managing standardized testing, there was little time devoted to counseling students about colleges and universities appropriate for their area of interest.

When planning this course for that semester, I could not have possibly imagined all that these undergraduate students would have learned through this partnership with a large urban high school. However, because I challenged them to think deeply about the questions they would need to ask to better understand the situation and setting, we gained invaluable insight into an issue of concern that challenges urban schools across the country—development of a college-going culture. So, while undergraduates were collaborating with high school students building raised beds for an urban garden, cleaning out an old greenhouse, and tutoring in biology, they were gaining skills and knowledge to support their understanding of urban schooling. Simultaneously, the high school students had a clearer plan for how to select colleges based on their interests and plans for the future and learned study skills for taking the AP Biology exam. Not to mention that both groups were discovering the benefits of urban gardening for communities living in food deserts. The high school biology students and the undergraduates mapped the community to learn where there were healthy food options (there were very few) and discussed the causes of food deserts in urban communities. Furthermore, they researched building a hydroponic garden and the plants that would grow best in that environment as well as which vegetables grow best in a raised bed. In this one semester, all these students not only gained physical skills, but they also gained skills of inquiry.

This experience served as the catalyst for my own queries into critical service-learning (CSL); Mitchell's (2008) work pushed me to think more about how I could plan my future courses in a more strategic manner to replicate this experience where my students had more room to influence both the curriculum and pedagogy of my course. I attempted to develop the course that centered undergraduates' experiences and knowledge so that we could build a curriculum around their expectations and potentially dismantle any preconceived notions or biases through service. Additionally, I endeavored to center the needs of the community partner so that their identified issues of concern would drive the course readings and development of an understanding of how they were under-resourced. After a few semesters, the ultimate goal for the course slowly became encouraging undergraduates to think critically about why organizations exist to meet the underserved needs of the members of the community and how schools also serve this role. This service experience informed all the subsequent semesters as I developed partnerships with schools and community organizations.

## Introducing the CSLIM

The CSLIM developed from one of these partnerships after 3 years of working with eighth graders engaging in their own CSL project at a local middle school (Coffey & Fulton, 2018). We align our definition of CSL with Mitchell's (2008) as a pedagogy and curriculum designed to "deconstruct systems of power so the need for service and the inequalities that create and sustain them are dismantled" (p. 50). The goal of CSL extends beyond fostering altruism and tolerance as are the typical desired outcomes for traditional service-learning models and challenges participants to focus on their potential as social change agents to respond to injustice within their communities and partnerships (Wade, 2000).

When Heather began partnering with public schools, she noted that service-learning was a popular pedagogy, especially in middle schools. As her own undergraduates mentored middle school students engaging in service-learning, Heather noticed that many of the same characteristics she observed in her university course were evident in the eighth-grade classrooms in which she was observing. Heather engaged in a formal research project with an eighth-grade English teacher who was implementing The Responsible Change Project, a service-learning curriculum supported by the language arts instruction. Over the course of a 3-year study working with middle school teachers who annually involve their eighth-grade students in The Responsible Change Project (Coffey & Fulton, 2018), a pattern of certain specific, recurrent practices similar to those identified by Mitchell (2008) began to emerge. Mitchell explained CSL builds on the work of the course, in this case, a yearlong unit on social justice and argument writing, to encourage a change in social orientation and develop as agents of change. In this particular case, these eighth-grade students were motivated to reflect and write about issues of concern they noticed within their communities while also researching the cause of similar injustices around the world. They were encouraged to seek information from community members, public servants, and nonprofit workers. As members of the community they were studying, these students did not appear to have a deficit view of the community; instead, they sought to investigate ways to make change by involving the members of the community.

As Heather observed the teacher's practice and the ways in which the students slowly gained confidence in calling local community agencies for information, she began noticing that the majority of the students were engaging in deep, critical discourse. The teacher was strategically having his students identify concerns within their communities, ask questions about how they might solve those concerns, collect data and research to formulate a way to advocate for change, and put that plan into action if possible. The teacher's pedagogical choice to introduce students to well-known international youth change agents and the concept of social justice early in the school year, coupled with a curriculum that supported writing research-based arguments, fostered student action for meaningful change in their communities. The teacher also transformed the traditional classroom space of rows and small groups into a more collaborative meeting space where students were trusted to meet in the school's makerspace, in the hallway, and were encouraged to partner with students in other English language arts classrooms on projects with similar interests.

Through observations of the teacher's classes and students, components of Mitchell's CSL began to emerge; Heather noticed the teacher was engaging in the following:

- "drawing attention to root causes of social problems, and involving students in actions and initiatives addressing root causes" (Mitchell, 2008, p. 51);
- encouraging students to see themselves as potential as agents for social change, and focus on injustice within their communities (Mitchell, 2008); and
- emphasizing community change over student outcomes.

After analyzing data from that school year, the findings suggested that middle school students were thinking deeply about social justice issues and considered themselves agents of change (Coffey & Fulton, 2020). Analysis of final projects indicated these students developed a sense of empathy for their community members who may not have had agency (Barnes & Coffey, 2021) and that they could think critically about the causes of the inequitable distribution of resources in their neighborhoods and city.

### *The Intersections of Critical Service-Learning and Critical Civic Empathy*

Drawing on the extant research in the field related to teacher practices in classrooms that engage in CSL (K–12), we began to think more deeply about how Mirra (2018) challenges us to (a) analyze the social position, power, and privilege of all people involved in the conversation; (b) focus on how personal experiences matter to each person and provides context for perspective; and (c) engage in "democratic dialogue and civic action committed to equity and justice" (p. 7). All these components are intended outcomes of our vision of CSL and provide us with a set of guidelines for evaluating our own practice.

CSLIM emerged from the partnership and guided our understanding of how K–12 classroom instruction and student engagement with the curriculum

might inform our own practice with CSL in the 2- and 4-year college setting. Heather developed an observation guide from her observations of her
undergraduates mentoring middle schoolers participating in the Responsible
Change Project; this guide included recurring characteristics or practices she
noticed during weekly observations across the semester. Heather organized
these characteristics into four major categories that included (1) *Pedagogy*
(teacher decision-making and practices), (2) *Observable student behaviors*
(i.e., interactions and practices), (3) *Space* (classroom layout and dynamics),
and (4) *Curriculum* (standards, activities, and lessons). In order to provide
interrater reliability on CSLIM, a graduate student familiar with the literature on CSL and Heather observed several lessons presented by two teachers.
After the lessons, they debriefed to compare notes on the characteristics of
CSL noticed during a week representative of the 50-minute class periods. On
each observation, there was a greater than 80% inter-rater reliability.

*Elements of CSLIM*

CSLIM is merely a model for exploring whether P–16 instructors might be
engaging in a practice of CSL and provides "look-fors" in four categories.
All these characteristics will not be present in each lesson or throughout the
curriculum. However, this model serves as a guide for thinking about how to
develop a curriculum that challenges service-learning participants to think
critically and a pedagogy that enables them to act.

In the following, we provide a list of the components of CSLIM and a more
detailed description of how pedagogy, space, curriculum, and student behaviors may work in tandem to create an opportunity for CSL. In the next
chapter, we describe each category and provide examples of how these components might look in K–12, university, and community college settings.

*Pedagogy.* We describe pedagogy as the planning and preparation of the
activities, lessons, and space related to teaching that includes CSL. In this section, we offer classroom exemplars to encourage a reflective process among
teachers and students engaging in the practice of CSL. CSLIM is not meant
to be an operationalized checklist but rather noticings from classroom nar-
ratives/stories that must focus on creating true community–university partnerships in which community issues and concerns are as important as student learning and development. In our experience teaching and observing

service-learning happening in real time, we have noticed that effective teacher planning and implementation in the area of CSL often include the following components:

- Community partner input and co-planning
- Evidence of reciprocal learning about difference and similarity (the instructor, community partner, and students learn about each other's culture and experience)
- Demonstration by the instructor of an understanding of student experience/background by referencing knowledge and making connections
- Strategic crafting by the instructor of activities to learn more about student experience/background
- Engagement by the instructor with students in guided and open-ended reflection
- Selection by the instructor of texts/experiences/opportunities that spark reflection on identity development
- Evidence that the instructor embraces the "progressive and liberal agenda" that undergirds CSL practice (Butin, 2015)
- Attempts by the instructor to raise critical consciousness (Freire, 1970)
- Students, instructors, and community partners are essential parts of formal and informal assessment
- Opportunities for dialogue, reflection, and writing assignments that encourage analysis of real-world concerns and push students to consider the systemic causes
- Opportunities for students to physically explore the community around the school/university and reflect on noticings
- Inclusion of presentations/co-teaching by community members/parents/stakeholders
- Use of careful/specific language by the instructor that does not promote deficit thinking and encourages students

*Space.* In order for CSL to be implemented in meaningful ways, we argue that the classroom space has to be arranged in a very different manner than a traditional classroom where student desks are organized in rows and the teacher lectures from the front. In fact, the learning and communication may not even take place inside the classroom. The following are the settings in which we have developed or noticed others developing a culture that supports CSL:

- May not look like a classroom or even be on campus (i.e., community partners often have meeting spaces where service providers/undergraduates can meet)
- Space offering opportunities for small-group and partner discussion
- Flexible seating, including couches, easily moved desks, and outdoor space
- Use of space suggesting mutuality: teacher and community partners as learner and learners as teacher and community partners
- Established environment in which it is obvious that students feel comfortable challenging their assumptions and speaking openly about difficult topics; students share personal information and thoughts even in the presence of an observer (more specifically mentors/tutors/community partners); everyone feels "safe"
- Students speaking their minds and respect their peers' opinions regardless of differences of opinion
- Opportunities for acknowledgment and acceptance of difference
- Opportunities for disequilibrium/discomfort
- Freedom in the learning environment (within reason) for students to move to comfortable spaces where they engage in paired, small-group, and large-group discussion
- Resources (i.e., telephones, computers, paper/pen) provided to communicate with community partners

*Curriculum.* Another powerful component of CSL is the carefully selected curriculum as the vehicle to challenge the status quo and promote developing a social justice mindset. Curriculum encompasses the activities, lessons, discussion and writing prompts, and standards related to the content. Service-learning employs a unique type of curriculum wherein students participate in a community engagement component with the goal of learning more about the people and the resources within that community. Over our years of teaching and observing others engaging CSL, we have noticed the following elements of curriculum that support this pedagogy:

- Curriculum focused on defining injustice, which may include words such as *bias, inequity, fairness, privilege, discrimination,* and *prejudice*
- Reframing strategies requiring the teacher and students to imagine themselves from another perspective are included
- Materials inviting questions about the distribution of power, including encouraging students to think about how the world would look if there was an equal distribution of money and resources
- Clarifying privilege including possible activities like the privilege walk and poverty simulation and classroom discussions about how privilege often influences the path of our lives
- Developing authentic relationships among students, faculty, and partners; teachers and students both exhibit comfort with each other in the discussion of difficult topics like race, poverty, and sexuality
- Challenging assumptions demonstrated with community partners, students, and teachers possibly asking the question, "Why do you believe this?" and/or offering a counterperspective
- Curriculum including a focus on social justice issues personal to the group; there are a variety of these but most commonly poverty, race, color, language, sexuality, orientation, gender, trafficking, DACA, and religious freedom
- The practice of problem posing (Freire, 1970) opposing the traditional method of teaching with the teacher as the vessel pouring knowledge into the students; in fact, the teacher serves more as a coach or guide asking the types of questions that challenge students' ability to critically engage with content and experiences
- Analyzing texts (informative and literary) for social issues as an element of the curriculum
- Pointing out power structures/hierarchies as a focus of the curriculum
- Confronting and reflecting on assumptions and stereotypes as a frequent practice
- Reliance on community-partner perspective for an accurate portrayal of group(s) being served

***Student Behaviors.*** This component of CSL is predicated on the idea that the teacher also considers themselves as a learner and that the students are empowered to engage in civic discourse. There is a sense of order and respect;

however, there is latitude to disagree and engage in informed argument. Student behaviors in a classroom that supports CSL may not reflect the typical classroom seen in American public schools. Our hope is that by setting guidelines and modeling how to engage in active listening, the instructor positions students in ways that center their interests and inquiry.

- Learners participate in small-group and paired discussions.
- Learners identify issues of concern within their communities.
- Learners develop functional and comprehensive definitions of agency and activism with real-world applications.
- Learners grapple with multiple perspectives.
- Learners challenge established beliefs and/or accepted "norms."
- Learners develop arguments using textual evidence.
- Learners create solutions/programs/education to advocate for causes.
- Learners act on evidence to create change.
- Learners present findings/research to a group of stakeholders.

## Implementing CSLIM

These components work together to create an opportunity for learners to question power relations, develop a deeper understanding for the community partner, and become comfortable with the idea of being advocates for change. In order for CSL to be enacted, we contend that the instructors, students, and community partners must all have a voice in determining the direction of the curriculum, pedagogy, space, and what this would look like for equity among all stakeholders. In fact, this model seeks to even out the power dynamics among faculty, students, and community partners by providing transparency for CSL and offering a structure for conversations. Although students and community partners may not enter these relationships with the same pedagogical experience as faculty, this tool provides the vocabulary necessary to create dialogue around curriculum, use of classroom space, pedagogy, and student behaviors. We would encourage practitioners to share the tool with all stakeholders early in a project and use it as a way to foster conversation throughout and beyond projects.

We do not suggest that this list is exhaustive and actually encourage researchers, faculty practitioners, CSL students, and community partners to add to and challenge this model for the advancement of the field. In the next chapter, we provide some additional context and detail for what that implementation might look like in both 4-year and 2-year college contexts.

## References

Butin, D. (2015). Dreaming of justice: Critical service-learning and the need to wake up. *Theory into Practice, 54*(1), 5–10. https://doi.org/10.1080/00405841.2015.977646

Barnes, M.E., & Coffey, H. (2021). Empowerment through rejection: Challenging divisions between traditional, authentic, and critical writing pedagogy. *English Teaching Practice & Critique, 20*(3), 313–327. https://doi.org/10.1108/ETPC-02-2020-0011

Coffey, H., & Fulton, S. (2018). The Responsible Change Project: Building a justice-oriented middle school curriculum through critical service-learning. *Middle School Journal, 49*(5), 16–25. https://doi.org/10.1080/00940771.2018.1509560

Coffey, H., & Fulton, S. (2020). The Responsible Change Project: Subverting the standardized English language arts curriculum. In J. Dyches, B. Sams, & A. Boyd (Eds.), *Acts of resistance: Subversive teaching in the ELA classroom* (pp. 110–122). Myers Educational Press.

Freire, P. (1970). *Pedagogy of the oppressed.* Seabury Press.

Mitchell, T. D. (2008, Spring). Traditional vs. critical service-learning: Engaging the literature to differentiate two models. *Michigan Journal of Community Service-Learning, 14*(2), 50–65. http://hdl.handle.net/2027/spo.3239521.0014.205

Mirra, N. (2018). *Educating for empathy: Literacy learning and civic engagement.* Teachers College Press.

Wade, R. (2000). Service-learning for multicultural teaching competency: Insights from the literature for teacher educators. *Equity & Excellence in Education, 121*, 21–29. https://doi.org/10.1080/1066568000330304

# The Critical Service-Learning Implementation Model in Action

A S WE DETAILED IN CHAPTER 3, the Critical Service-Learning Implementation Model (CSLIM) was developed out of our interest in learning what critical service-learning (CSL) looks like in practice on a variety of levels. After conducting years of empirical research related to the benefits of service-learning for undergraduate students and community partners, we saw a need to clearly define what differentiated CSL from traditional service-learning. Through our observations of eighth graders at a public middle school and our own experiences teaching service-learning courses, we focused on four areas of import: Pedagogy (teacher planning), Space, Curriculum, and Student Behaviors (habits/attitudes/dispositions). In what follows, we further articulate what this practice of CSL looks like through these four components.

## Pedagogy and Teacher Planning

Using critical pedagogical methods, teachers create spaces where they can be learners and students can be teachers, thus providing a context for everyone to construct and interrogate theories of knowledge. Freire (1970) offers an example of how students become more socially aware and empowered through a critique of injustice. This awareness cannot be achieved if students are not given the opportunity to explore and construct knowledge. We posit that CSL opposes the "banking" model of education where learners are viewed as "'receptacles' to be 'filled' by the teachers" (Freire, 1970, p. 72). In these classrooms, "knowledge is a gift bestowed by those who consider themselves knowledgeable upon those whom they consider to know nothing," (Freire, 1970, p. 72) and the teachers separate themselves as being the possessors of knowledge. In this role, the teacher does not necessarily challenge the students to think critically or value prior knowledge students bring to the learning environment. In opposition to the banking model, teachers who recognize the potential value of critical pedagogy offer experiences for knowledge construction and analysis. In this model, schools become spaces where students interrogate social conditions through dialogue about issues significant to their lives. We argue that CSL, like critical literacy, positions teachers as facilitators of dialogue that question traditional power relations. Additionally, we argue that the community must become a part of this pedagogy and that stakeholders and community partners must be given the opportunity to learn from students while students conversely learn from them.

Planning the actual unit of instruction is a crucial factor for successfully implementing CSL (see Table 4.1). Faculty hoping to engage in CSL must strategically activate students' prior knowledge and understandings at the beginning of the unit (or even the school year/semester) in order to set the stage for the outcomes of the unit. Instructors must identify anticipated outcomes early and develop activities, lessons, experiences, and so on that facilitate the direction in which CSL progresses. In the classroom that uses CSL, similarly to a classroom that engages critical pedagogy, students begin to take over the development of new knowledge and the planning of the curriculum through their interactions with community partners; in some cases, the service-learning project is designed by the learners in collaboration with the service recipients, based on the needs identified by the service recipients. Often, there is even pushback from students as they struggle or wobble with taking control of their own learning (Coffey & Barnes, 2021). CSL looks very messy as it does not reflect what some might refer to as "traditional" teaching methods. For some additional details and suggestions on syllabus development and goal alignment, see Chapter 5.

Over the course of the unit, the CSL facilitator incrementally encourages students to take more control of the activities and knowledge development while building relationships with the community partner. Ideally, students will guide the direction of the service-learning on identifying an issue of concern and critical analysis of structural inequities.

*Community College Examples: Lucy's Story*

One challenge I faced in teaching at the community college was the use of a department-wide syllabus, course shell, and curricula components. This impacted my teaching in some specific ways in composition courses; for example, I was required to assign four essays in four learning modules intended to be taught in a particular order. When I first began teaching at one institution,

Table **4.1.** Pedagogy—The Planning and Preparation of the Activities, Lessons, and Space

| |
|---|
| **Evidence of reciprocal learning** about difference and similarity (the instructor, students, and community partner learn about each other's culture and experience) |
| **Instructor demonstration of understanding of student experience/background** by referencing knowledge and making connections |
| **Strategically crafted activities** to learn more about student and community partner experience/background |
| **Student engagement in guided and open-ended reflection** |
| **Instructor-, community partner-, and student-selected texts/experiences/opportunities** that spark reflection on identity development |
| **Evidence instructor embraces the "progressive and liberal agenda"** that undergirds critical service-learning practice (Butin, 2006) |
| **An obvious attempt to raise critical consciousness** (Freire, 1970) |
| **Collaborative informal and formal planning** |
| **Opportunities for dialogue, reflection, and writing assignments that encourage analysis** of real-world concerns and push students to consider the systemic causes |
| **Opportunities for students to physically explore the community** around the school/university/service setting and reflect on noticings |
| **Inclusion of presentations/coteaching by community partners/parents/stakeholders** |
| **Use and encouragement of careful language that promotes asset-based perspectives** |

I was required to teach and assign a rhetorical analysis for the first assignment. I am not going to get into the whole discussion around composition courses and the teaching of rhetoric, but suffice it to say, there is an ongoing conversation there. For my part, I find rhetorical analysis to be a challenging starting point for new college students, particularly students in English 101 at the community college. The first assignment in a composition course matters quite a bit because it impacts the momentum and feelings of efficacy of new college students. At the community college, although I always had a number of students right out of high school who had been successful enough in school, I also generally had students who had struggled in high school, students who had been out of school for years (from 1 to 30 years), and many students who just weren't sure they were going to be able to hack it in college. How they felt about and performed on that first writing assignment was crucial.

I tried a few iterations of rhetorical analysis to try to make the concept more accessible for my students, but it was really a CSL approach to teaching that set me on a path that meant something more to my students and ultimately to me. I developed an assignment called "A Rhetoric of Place" and asked students to think about how particular places were designed and what those design choices suggested about the attitudes of designers toward users. We used our classrooms at the college as a starting place. We studied the narrow windows, the institutional paint jobs, the antiquated technology, the teacher and student spaces, and the flow of the buildings to try to understand what designers of these spaces intended for us as students and teachers. We also considered the ways in which we as users played along with these design choices and the ways in which we hacked those designs. After these initial sessions of co-constructing meaning about our institutional spaces, students were encouraged to consider and write about other spaces as well, though they all had the opportunity to continue inquiring into and writing about classroom spaces as well.

This example highlights how it is possible to apply a CSL pedagogy, even when some curriculum is mandated (which is the case in some community college and 4-year college settings). This assignment encourages reciprocal learning; while a study of rhetoric often situates the instructor as the expert, by encouraging students to inquire into spaces about which they are expert users, that power imbalance changes. Students were learning about rhetoric from me, but I was learning about how they thought of, used, and hacked spaces from them. We co-constructed that learning. This assignment also values and prioritizes students' funds of knowledge and the rich background experiences they bring to classroom contexts. As I describe in greater detail earlier, this assignment was specifically crafted to bring student expertise and experience to their learning and writing.

Guided reflections served as precursors to students' own rhetoric of place writings. Geared toward identity development, this assignment was designed to help students think about how their identities are informed by institutional decisions while also exploring areas where they can contest those predetermined ideas about identity. I intentionally crafted this assignment to espouse a more progressive mindset and to spark critical thinking, awareness, and conversation among students. The heart of the work is developing critical consciousness around public spaces. Although I crafted this sequence and assignment as the faculty member, I did include students and community members in conversations as we worked; everyone was welcome to make meaning from this writing for their own ends; that said, this is an area of reflection for me as an instructor. In what ways can I include students and community members in the development of activities and assignments?

This assignment successfully encourages students to consider the impacts of institutions on their lives and experiences, which prepares them to consider systemic causes. Students are also encouraged to carefully consider place, and although many students continue to study school settings, others consider public and private spaces in their communities. This assignment sequence includes informal presentations and thinking from community members, including the librarians, teachers, park rangers, and other community members who are drawn into the inquiries and discussions as the work continues. Avoiding deficit language about users of spaces is a crucial element of this activity and one that leads to awareness of how pervasive deficit thinking about users is in public spaces.

*Undergraduate Settings Examples: Heather's Story*

Similarly, undergraduate students must be given opportunities to develop critical consciousness by learning more about the communities in which they will serve and use their knowledge to support initiatives within those communities. Instructors teaching in 4-year colleges and universities arguably have more flexibility in their pedagogical methods and may find this setting more conducive to CSL. Although they may not be native to the community surrounding the university, undergraduates have the ability to go out into the community to develop relationships in order to learn more about issues of concern. Furthermore, community partners are welcome to come to campus and share about their organizations and a facilitate deeper understanding of how they support underserved community members.

At the university level, like in the community college environment, we must strive to meet learning objectives for each course. One such course is described in the introduction to Chapter 3; this service-learning course primarily focuses on critical issues in education. The majority of students who enroll in my course plan to work in careers that serve the public interest such as teaching counseling, nursing, and criminal justice. In order to facilitate a CSL pedagogy, I have established partnerships with organizations in close proximity to the university so that students develop a sense of community and better understand the needs of the people living beyond the physical walls of the campus. These community partners have the opportunity to come to campus to discuss their goals and mission, and similarly, students do not have to travel far to see the population the organizations are serving. Together, with the community organizations, I develop the curriculum, encouraging their input into how to approach the integration of community voice into the foundation of the course. For example, I have taught this course in extra space on a middle school campus (partner) so that undergraduates could learn more about the culture of the school. When the schedule changed at the university and the course was split between biweekly meetings, I worked with the community partners, in this case middle school teachers, to figure out how we would build trust with eighth-grade students. The teacher had been using FlipGrid to engage his students with their service-learning projects, so the undergraduates and I learned the technology in order to communicate and build relationships with our eighth-grade community partners without actually having to go to their campus each week. Thus, I began to depend on my community partner, a middle school teacher, to help develop my course/pedagogy prior to the beginning of the semester so that we could go into the semester having identified goals for the partnership.

### Teacher Preparation Program Example

In our experience with CSL within a middle school setting, we noted that CSL calls to mind the work of Freire (1970) in that teachers essentially sought to facilitate the development of critical consciousness with their students through the use of critical pedagogy. More specifically, this example highlights a particular group of teachers who were engaging critical literacy through examining texts that presented differing perspectives of a selected issue. These teachers began planning prior to the start of the school year with the overarching goal of engaging students in a yearlong progression of activities, readings, writing assignments, and discussions that enabled students to question issues of concern in their communities and to research possible solutions for making grassroots change. The team of teachers we observed over a 3-year period very carefully selected literature, informational texts, TEDTalk videos, and other forms of media to introduce the concept of activism and advocacy. The goal of the yearlong unit was to introduce students to the concept of social justice, engage them in research on a topic of interest, and show them what youth agency looks like. All this was done in the hopes of engendering a sense of agency among these students so they would feel comfortable expressing their own perspectives and taking action. In one particular instance, the students sought out community partners based on their concerns about issues within their communities. Essentially, student interest drove the research and writing in this CSL example, and students sought partnerships with community organizations in their quest for more information and to make change.

## Space

The category of Space is closely linked to the category of Pedagogy in the model we envision for CSL. In the case of the Responsible Change Project, the first year and a half that Heather observed students and teachers, they met in an overcrowded classroom where desks were arranged in three-person pods. Students were actually encouraged to work with peers with similar interests in other English language arts (ELA) classes that met at the same time, so they were often moving between two classrooms on opposite ends of a long hall. They took their Chromebooks into the hallways where they would huddle in small groups or pairs searching for research or programs that would give them ideas about how to address their concerns. Heather's undergraduates met at the middle school each Friday morning and had class for an hour; then they joined the eighth graders on the floor in the hallways or in the library to discuss their research and projects for the remaining 2 hours of class. Oftentimes, the teachers would take time away from the day's planned activities to address common concerns voiced by the students. In these moments, students would pile into one classroom and sit on cabinets by the windows or could be found sitting "crisscross applesauce" in the corners of the room where there was no available seating in the form of desks. The ELA teachers would "tag team" the concerns with all 52 students in one space; they would answer questions or problem-solve with students on issues that seemed to emerge overwhelmingly. Early in her teaching at the university, Heather realized that the best way for her students to get to know the needs of the community was to go to the community sites and learn directly from the partners. The "space" of the university definitely did not compare to the opportunities to be in the community.

As an aside, during the first couple years of this particular research project, a new middle school was being constructed, and the teachers were given the opportunity to provide input about the types of space they would need for instruction, activities, and collaboration. In response, the architects and administrators provided flexible meeting space in the form of an outdoor quad for whole-group meetings, a grade-level lounge with flexible seating and ample whiteboards for planning, and the crowning jewel, a makerspace for small-group interaction and experimenting with materials for solutions to community problems. These flexible spaces, specifically included in the building design, were included to encourage collaboration, innovative pedagogy, and creativity, all of which are perfect for CSL. (See Table 4.2.)

Table 4.2. Space—Both the Physical Space and How It Engenders Agency

| Opportunities for small-group and partner discussion |
| --- |
| **Flexible Seating** includes nontraditional classroom furniture, easily moved desks, outdoor space |
| **Mutuality** (teacher as learner and learner as teacher) |
| **Trust/Safety** (The teacher has established an environment where it is obvious students feel comfortable challenging their assumptions and speaking openly about difficult topics. Students share personal information and thoughts even in the presence of an observer. Everyone feels "safe".) |
| **Respect** (Regardless of differences of opinion, students speak their mind and respect their peers' opinions.) |
| **Acknowledgment and acceptance** of difference as a benefit |
| **Opportunity for disequilibrium/discomfort** |
| **Mutual understanding of goals** (Within lessons and activities, the students appear to understand what is expected of them and the teacher looks to the students to help develop goals.) |
| **Fluidity/Flexibility** (Within the learning environment, students have the opportunity to change their minds about topics/opinions without worrying they will fall behind. Students understand that they must always have a backup plan.) |

*Undergraduate Examples: Heather's Story*

My campus has definitely focused on having a flexible space for supporting undergraduate learning. In fact, several buildings have active learning classrooms that support easy transitions into pairs and groups, multiple whiteboard/writing surfaces to brainstorm and plan, access to technology, and SMART podiums for presentations. When I had the opportunity to use these spaces to teach the service-learning course, there seemed to be more flexibility with collaboration instead of when students were bound by rows and immovable chalkboards (yes, chalkboards in 2019!).

Although these courses were often taught in small, traditional, windowless classrooms, I was still able to engage students in using outdoor spaces and the library for offering students areas to collaborate and talk in small groups. At the beginning of each semester, I scheduled team-building activity sessions with the campus outdoor leadership program. In these sessions, trained facilitators engaged students in problem-solving and team-building activities so that participants would begin to trust one another, develop communication and negotiation skills, and learn to work together to solve problems. These sessions set the tone for the semester as I wanted to center the curriculum on the students' questions about the community partners with whom they would be working. Additionally, students were able to move around and interact with the environment, which encouraged them to think of themselves as members of a community.

### Community College Examples: Lucy's Story

In *Critical Teaching and Everyday Life* (1980), Shor discusses the institutional spaces of community colleges, a strategy that I incorporate in my Rhetoric of Place unit in first-year composition at the community college. The physical spaces of community college classrooms vary in terms of flexibility; in some spaces, desks and chairs are movable, and in other locations, they just aren't. I have had some luck with moving to other campus locations, like the learning commons or outdoor common areas (weather permitting). These changes in meeting spaces reflect opportunities to change thinking spaces and relationships as well; alternate meeting locations can make teacher and student positioning murkier, with opportunities for students to demonstrate expertise over the spaces in ways that it is often more challenging for them to do in traditional classroom spaces where teachers have the login credentials for the computers and students are used to teachers dominating the spaces.

I often facilitate these sorts of shifts in power dynamics by setting up student groups prior to transitions; then students are empowered to shape the spaces as they wish when they convene. For example, students read excerpts from Peter Elbow's (1998) *Writing Without Teachers*, write agendas, and write drafts in order to prepare for writing groups. Then, I encourage the writing groups to meet in alternate spaces. Some groups prefer to sit outside and work together, while others choose to use learning commons spaces with computers to facilitate Google Doc commenting. Even when activities are happening in the traditional classroom, ways of organizing the physical space can encourage the development of authentic relationships and shift power dynamics (Mitchell, 2008), components of mutuality. Organizing desks into circles, using small-group activities, and facilitating student presentations are ways of hacking traditional spaces to encourage those alternate mindsets. Trust and safety undergird all these types of activities.

Over the past year, I have started using a syllabus statement that states support for traditionally marginalized students, including Black students and trans students. Establishing clear language and a sense of community from the first day of the semester encourages trust, community, and respect. I encourage students to use practices I learned from nonviolent communication (NVC) via the work of Dr. Marshall Rosenberg. These practices include naming feelings and needs and making requests as needed. For example, I might say, "When I hear someone say that a particular song is 'gay,' meaning bad in some way, my need for safety and respect as a queer person is not being met. Would you all be willing to stop using 'gay' in that particular way?" I encourage students to use that same kind of communication with each other and offer coaching as necessary. These NVC strategies are not meant to eliminate discomfort; sometimes, topics covered in the class are uncomfortable, and I am more interested in encouraging students to understand their own reactions, empathize with others, and communicate effectively about their needs.

## Curriculum

Integrating a CSL approach requires careful consideration of how pedagogy and space influence the ways in which students experience the curriculum. (See Table 4.3.) We recommend that faculty craft meaningful activities, constantly informed by feedback from community partners. Service-learning participants also rely on the community partners to help them better understand their needs so that they can work to help them meet the needs.

Table 4.3. Curriculum—Activities, Assignments, and Standards for Critical Service-Learning

| Curriculum: Classroom Activities/Discussions/Lessons |
| --- |
| **Defining Injustice** (might also be transposed with inequity/unfairness/injustice/discrimination/bias/prejudice) |
| **Reframing** requires the teacher or student to imagine themselves from another perspective |
| **Questioning** the distribution of power would include having students to think about how the world would look if there was an equal distribution of money and resources |
| **Clarifying** privilege might include activities like the privilege walk and poverty simulation, classroom discussions about how people are born with certain privileges |
| **Developing** authentic relationships among students, faculty, and partners. The teachers and students both exhibit comfort with each other in the discussion of difficult topics like race, poverty, sexuality. |
| **Challenging** assumptions might be demonstrated with students and teachers asking the question, "Why do you believe this?" or offering a counterperspective |
| **Focusing** on social justice issues that are personal to the group. There are a variety of these, but the most common are poverty, race, color, language, sexuality, orientation, gender, trafficking, DACA, religious freedom. |
| **Posing** questions that might challenge students' understanding of their experience and understanding of the world |
| **Analyzing** texts (informative and literary) for social issues |
| **Pointing** out power structures/hierarchies |
| **Confronting** assumptions and stereotypes |
| **Accepting privilege** admitting that sometimes privilege is a part of circumstance and that some people benefit from circumstances they had no control over (i.e., skin color, income of parents) |
| **Reflecting and Writing** about the ways in which mindsets/opinions may have changed due to knowledge gained through experience |

## Community College Examples: Lucy's Story

One of my goals as a teacher is to be as in the moment as possible when I am teaching and working with students and in our communities. I'm a cerebral person, and I've often found myself challenged to really listen and respond in that moment rather than connecting to my past research and reading or thinking ahead to my next step or goal. CSL requires that attention to people in the moment in order to develop those authentic relationships and to orient us toward social change. An example of how this related to curriculum occurred in a CSL composition course I taught that was primarily composed of men of color; this was the enrollment goal for the course, which was intended to be taught by a Black male professor. Things never go as they are planned at any institution where I've taught, and a variety of students ended up being added to the course in the end, and I ended up teaching it, even though I am White and a cis-gendered woman. In order to begin our discussions of privilege, I began with race, because that was the way the course was recruited, at least initially. What does it mean to be Black? This question yielded such complexity and fraught thought and emotion, and it was a conversation that continued throughout the semester, through discussions about Black men, colorism, police reform, attitudes toward queer people, and many more topics. It was important to me to avoid having my opinions or perspectives become dominant, despite my position as a professor. I had to walk a line between a sort of radical vulnerability about my own queerness and experience as the mom of a Black child and active listening, asking questions, and building community among students.

One of the most successful strategies I used with this class was the introduction of small reading groups. The groups selected a short reading on a topic related to an area of interest and then discussed it together without my mitigation. Then, when we came back together as a whole class, I modeled asking the students questions about their articles and responses. Eventually, other students took over with the questions asking and problem posing.

*Undergraduate Examples: Heather's Story*

Developing curriculum to support undergraduate students engaging in service-learning courses in a liberal arts program is not overly challenging. For the most part, university instructors have autonomy in curriculum development for prerequisite-level undergraduate courses. Integrating the characteristics of CSL into any content area would merely require a focus on inquiry related to systemic injustice and social justice issues. In my courses, after fostering a sense of community through team-building activities and improvisation games, I explain that the first few weeks of the class will include a more structured focus on defining social justice and engaging in community-based research. In order to learn more about their community partners and the issues they identify as problematic, undergraduates complete critical reflections, community mapping, and a social justice inquiry project, and then, they collaborate with their community partners to identify one issue of focus where they can create a legacy for future undergraduates partnering with the community organization. After some initial teacher-directed instruction, the curriculum shifts to focus on the needs of the community partner, and I expect undergraduates to lead activities and find readings to support their inquiry. Admittedly, undergraduates are extremely uncomfortable with taking leadership in building the course curriculum; however, I find that student-led activities and discussions are essential components of CSL.

The curriculum for my service-learning course includes brainstorming/ mind mapping, community mapping, a social justice project, and the course concludes with a legacy project, which is how I bridge the issue of semester time limitations and community partnerships. This legacy project is a non-negotiable component of the course curriculum; however, it develops out of conversations and problem-posing between the community partner and the undergraduates. I do not have many requirements except that there is a physical outcome (i.e., a fundraiser, a guidebook, or a web resource) born out of the needs of the community partners and a presentation of what was learned through the experience and how the project can support or inform the work of the next semester of undergraduates engaging in the partnership. In past years, undergraduates in my classes have sponsored a spaghetti dinner to raise funds for new linens for a temporary homeless shelter at a community partner location, developed a website for undergraduate student organizations to volunteer to prepare and distribute bagged lunches for the homeless living in the city, and prepared a web tutorial for future volunteers with the Responsible Change Project at a local middle school. Although all these outcomes were representative of a more traditional model of service-learning, students did have to include a personal reflection related to what they learned about social justice and inequality through their service and how community partners informed their development of projects.

## Student Behaviors

As mentioned earlier, Heather observed eighth-grade ELA students participating in the Responsible Change Project (Coffey & Fulton, 2018) over a 3-year period. During this time, the eighth graders actively engaged in a range of behaviors (see Table 4.4), and they were given freedom by their teachers to develop solutions to "problems" they observed within their communities as part of the National Writing Project's College, Career, and Community Writing Program (C3WP; see Coffey & Fulton, 2018). Each year, throughout the course of the project, students worked collaboratively in small groups and pairs, as well as individually, to research an issue of concern and to develop potential solutions with a community partner.

During this time, students began to identify major concerns within their communities (i.e., gun violence, animal abuse, a lack of Spanish language translation for local government–sponsored web resources). Not only did these eighth graders point out these issues, but they also researched the topic using primary documents and social media resources. They respectfully engaged in discourse with their classmates on issues on which they did not always agree. There were heated moments, but these students adhered to the expectations of respect while delivering their arguments through debate, writing assignments, and classroom discussions. As students were exposed to a variety of social justice issues happening around the country, they were expected to research the multiple perspectives connected to those issues. This learning took place through a recursive series of lessons that focused on reading informational texts, developing nuanced claims, connecting claims to evidence, and developing written arguments that comment on material from multiple sources. This process developed a classroom culture of argument (not always negative), in which students learned to listen, consider different viewpoints, and ask critical questions or engage in discourse, in addition to learning about argument writing and current events. (See Table 4.4.) During this time, students developed classroom community and honed the skill of civil discourse, a skill they will need as adult citizens in a democracy. Furthermore, these students learned valuable skills of drafting an email or a script to call a public official or community leader and collaborating with those community organizations to make change. These eighth-grade students mirrored similar behaviors as college students tasked with similar goals for learning.

*Community College Examples: Lucy's Story*

In my community college composition courses, I encourage students to examine, research, and engage with social issues in their communities. At my college, particular numbers and types of essays are required, so, in order to meet that requirement, I have students first research a selected social issue for one essay and then propose a solution for a second essay. To begin the process, students brainstorm issues in their communities in small groups and then circulate the room, adding ideas to lists developed by other groups of students. Students then select inquiry groups around shared research topics. These shared inquiry groups, in addition to collaborating on service-learning activities, create shared annotated bibliographies, an activity that scaffolds a research assignment first-year students often struggle with initially. Student inquiry groups work on common service-learning activities related to their selected topics. Their engagement with communities encourages them to think about solutions collaboratively and with input and context from community members. For example, in a recent semester, one group of students became interested in high-needs public elementary schools and achievement, while another group studied housing instability in the area around our campus. The first group talked to school administrators at a local elementary school and used their input on both their inquiry project and their CSL project. The second group coordinated with two homeless shelter nonprofits in the area to supplement their research on housing instability and then used their research to develop ideas for sustainable CSL projects. Their research and service-learning inform their final essay on solutions. This sequence of assignments meets college student learning outcomes, as well as encouraging student activism and community engagement.

**Table 4.4.** Observable Student Behaviors—Practices and Habits Exhibited by Students Participating in Critical Service-Learning

| |
|---|
| Small group and paired **discussion** |
| **Identification** of issues of concern within community/society |
| Development of functional and comprehensive definition of **agency** and **activism** with real-world application |
| **Grappling** with multiple perspectives |
| **Challenging** established beliefs and/or accepted "norms" |
| **Developing** arguments using textual evidence |
| **Creating** solutions/programs/education to advocate for a cause |
| **Acting** on evidence to create change |
| **Presenting** findings/research to a group/groups of stakeholders, community partners, and/or decision-makers |

*Undergraduate Examples: Heather's Story*

In the university setting, undergraduates quickly learn that they are expected to participate in collaborative group assignments and to engage in inquiry. At my large public university, there is a strong commitment to developing skills of inquiry, communication, and critical thought. As such, I have piloted many of the courses that combine all these skills into a variety of content areas. As a result of teaching these courses, I have introduced many of these skills into her service-learning courses and found that they support CSL. Undergraduate students often shy away from disagreements or debate with classmates at the beginning of the semester, but once they understand how to support their perspectives with research and facts, they are more likely to engage in argument-based discourse respectfully.

Another practice that undergraduates are timid about is communicating their ideas or solutions to concerns they have with stakeholders. When I first have students identify a social justice issue that affects these first- and second-year students, they have a difficult time articulating a potential solution to someone who could potentially make a difference. An example of this occurred in 2019 when one student was specifically concerned about her own mental health associated with the stress of navigating all the decisions of becoming an adult in college. She was dealing with anxiety and could not schedule an appointment with the counseling services because her own course schedule did not align with their hours of operation. She expressed sincere discontent about this issue inside the safe space of the classroom and was met with nodding heads and similar stories. When this problem was posed to the class, they came up with the solution to talk to the dean of students about the potential of extended hours for counseling services. Although it took a couple weeks to finally schedule an appointment with this stakeholder, she presented her case to him in a logical manner using data and research she had conducted about college students and anxiety. This first-year college student not only identified an issue of concern for herself; she also presented evidence to support her argument on a social justice issue that many first-year college students grapple with.

These behaviors and patterns are not simply assigned to maturation into adulthood, they represent recognition of one's role as a contributing member of society/community. Furthermore, we contend that engaging in CSL has the potential to help K–16 students build confidence and agency in ways that traditional service-learning does not necessarily support.

## Practical Applications and Next Steps for CSLIM

As these examples demonstrate, the strength of this model is the concrete opportunities that it offers to foster conversations about CSL among faculty, students, and community partners. The success of CSL is about moving toward a more socially just world, so creating these power dynamic–aware opportunities for input and conversation are crucial to our work.

In the next two chapters, we offer actionable suggestions for CSL practitioners; in Chapter 5, we review strategies for planning CSL in alignment with Table 4.1 of the model. In Chapter 6, we review reflective cycles that incorporate elements in alignment with Tables 4.2, 4.3, and 4.4.

## References

Coffey, H., & Barnes, M. (2021). Wobbling with culturally proactive teaching: Facilitating social justice through youth participatory action research with middle school students. *Teachers College Record, 123*(13). https://www.tcrecord.org/library

Coffey, H., & Fulton, S. (2018). The Responsible Change Project: Building a justice-oriented middle school curriculum through critical service-learning. *Middle School Journal, 49*(5), 16–25. https://doi.org/10.1080/00940771.2018.1509560

Elbow, P. (1998). *Writing without teachers* (2nd ed.). Oxford University Press.

Freire, P. (1970). *Pedagogy of the oppressed*. Seabury Press.

Mitchell, T. D. (2008, Spring). Traditional vs. critical service-learning: Engaging the literature to differentiate two models. *Michigan Journal of Community Service-Learning, 14*(2), 50–65. http://hdl.handle.net/2027/spo.3239521.0014.205

Shor, I. (1980). *Critical teaching & everyday life*. University of Chicago Press.

# FIVE

# Planning for Identity Exploration With Critical Service-Learning

IN THIS CHAPTER, WE EXPLORE some of the ways faculty can effectively plan for critical service-learning (CSL) projects and activities and consider how frontloading discussions around identity might foster CSL work.

## Lucy's Story

Drawing on Jack Halberstam's (2011) opus on queer failure, I'm going to begin this chapter with a story of failing. The first time I stood in front of a course I taught with a CSL focus, I had a very clear idea of what the semester was going to look like. I had studied CSL and planned very carefully. I knew that we would bond as a class and then we would come up with a focus and a direction for our service project and activities. I imagined that the project would conclude right around the end of the semester, and everything would be neatly tied up.

As it turned out, none of these prognostications came true—at least not in the ways I imagined them. From the beginning, the class-bonding experience was challenging. There were arguments about "color blindness," with many students arguing that being colorblind was a solid way to solve racism. One of the most activist-oriented students also turned out to be grappling with transphobia. We struggled to come to agreement about a project or a community partner. In the end, the project did conclude at the end of the semester, but that wasn't really a positive outcome; we didn't have a clear plan to continue that work. Despite my best efforts and research, I'm not sure, if we were to apply the Critical Service-Learning Implementation Model (CSLIM) to my class that semester, we would even argue that it was CSL.

Students show up at college for a lot of different reasons, and they are coming from all kinds of experiences and backgrounds. That's the exciting thing about teaching college, especially first-year students, and the confounding thing. I think about that particular semester often when I'm planning my courses now because it reminds me of many important things about planning a CSL course. One, students are not a monolith. Even when courses are in the major or taught for third or fourth-year students, they are all different from each other and from me. Doing CSL does not mean bringing us all into alignment. It means being able to sit with our differences and our discomforts and to find productive ways to talk about them. Luckily for all of us, social change doesn't depend on our lockstep agreement; it depends on our cooperation, our ability to communicate, and our love for each other.

## Heather's Story

For the last 12 years, I have taught a service-learning class for mostly preservice teacher candidates at least once a semester in a large public university. This course really is something I look forward to each semester as it gives me the opportunity to plant one foot firmly in the community while keeping the other on campus. As a teacher at heart, I miss the excitement of the middle school setting and the energy curious minds bring to class, and this course gives me the chance to return to my roots as a public school teacher. The last time I taught this particular course, although there was a palpable change in the ways in which I was able to connect with my students and with community partners. The university altered the course schedule so that I went from meeting for three hours on a Friday morning to meeting 1.5 hours 2 days per week. This change in schedule truly disrupted my ability to build community and engage students in exploring their own identities.

Additionally, a course that meets on Friday morning at 9:30 for 3 hours seems to attract a different kind of student than one that meets for a very short time in the middle of the week. For reasons I haven't yet explored, the majority of undergraduates in this particular group did not read the course description and were unaware that I required 30 hours of service outside of the class meeting time. These students were not representative of my previous students, and very few planned to become teachers. In fact, their identities were bound up in becoming business or communications majors, which, as it turns, out did not require them to focus too much on issues of social justice. In order to connect their service in the course with their future careers, we did an exercise in predicting how much they would make in their first year working in the marketing field or in an entry-level position for the bank as compared to becoming a teacher. Afterward, when the shock of the disparity between teacher and corporate salaries wore off, we began to focus on how our identities lead us to our career choices and how those careers give us leverage to fight for social justice from a variety of perspectives. I would love to follow up with this group of students one day to see where their journeys have taken them and how many of them actually still serve their communities. There are many changes I would make prior to teaching this course in this particular structure again; all these changes revolve around critical reflection and building stronger activities with community partners.

## Strategies for Applying CSL

One understanding that faculty new to service-learning of any stripe bring is that service-learning is an additive pedagogy; that is, that to include service-learning in a syllabus, faculty must make space for it through compression or deletion of other course content. A key idea is that CSL is not additive in this sense; instead, CSL is a mindset that pervades all aspects of the course, from development through implementation. CSL is not, then, just another thing to teach; CSL is a way to teach the content you are already adapting.

In this chapter, we discuss the concept of identity and its relationship to CSL, the strengths of community connections, relational connections to content, and how to develop a CSL-oriented syllabus.

### Identity and CSL

Because we've already established the need for commitment to social justice and equity as a starting point for CSL faculty, the next question for us is, How does CSL help you and your students meet the learning goals for the course? In order to answer this question, we need to think about theories of identity and how those understandings of identity tie in with learning.

Gergen (2009) provides some helpful examples for understanding how relationships develop identities:

Consider that:
- If a policeman says "Stop where you are." . . . you become a suspect.
- If a salesperson says, "Can I help you?" . . . you become a customer.
- If your wife says, "Can you give me a hand, honey?" . . . you become a husband.
- If a child says, "Mommy come quick." . . . you become a mother.

Others call us into being as a suspect, a customer, a husband, a mother, and so on. Would we be any of these without such callings? (p. 38).

In classroom settings, some aspects of our identities as students and teachers are already in place, and we have to actively consider how we might subvert those identities in order to do CSL. For example, in order to both develop authentic relationships and contest power dynamics, we have to be willing to shift power dynamics in the classroom, where faculty generally wield power over students. Casting ourselves as co-learners with our students in the Freirean sense is one way we do this. We talk more about crafting a syllabus later in this chapter.

Crucially, in order for students to participate in CSL activities, they need to engage in self-awareness reflections and activities. They may have accepted some aspects of their identities and eschewed others, either consciously or unconsciously; in order to partner with others for social change, they will need to understand their own choices and biases. In Chapter 6, we cover some tools for reflection that will be useful in this process. Here are some other activities that might help.

*Privilege Walk/Exploration.* There are a number of online sources to help facilitate this activity. The general idea is students line up (preferably outside or in a large space). The facilitator calls out an attribute that causes each student to either step forward or backward, for example, "if you are right-handed, take a step forward" or "if you have ever had to skip a meal because you didn't have access to food, step backward." This activity is uncomfortable and encourages students to consider privilege in a variety of ways. We have sometimes paired this activity with McIntosh's (1989) "White Privilege: Unpacking the Invisible Knapsack", depending on the group and their particular needs.

In another version of this activity, we give students beads and string, and they make a "privilege bracelet" as they think through facets of their own identity. They go through the exercise focusing on nationality, sexuality, religion, class, race, ability, biological sex, and gender, all of which make up major parts of their identity. Then, we ask these students to reflect on privilege rather than on oppression and marginalization. We also guide them through a discussion about the intersectionality of their identities and how we, as instructors, also have to navigate and sometimes hide (deny, justify, ignore) our privilege on a daily basis.

*Identity illustration.* To participate in this activity, students need to understand that there are many aspects of identity that create privilege, and all of that depends on context. This activity can be done as a freeform drawing or art project in which students depict elements of their identity; Lucy has been using an Interactive Identity Wheel created by the Teacher Professional Development Group Science Museum of Minnesota (2015), which she encountered through the Branch Alliance for Educator Diversity. This digital tool provides sliders on a number of identity spectrums, including sexual orientation, race, socioeconomic class, disability, gender, religion or spiritual beliefs, age, language, and family composition.

Additionally, Heather has students watch videos about how parents are the primary influencer of how their children view society and then explore topics of interest related to identity development through *Identiversity: Gender and Sexual Identity Learning Hub* (https://www.identiversity.org/). Heather then guides students in a discussion about how the lens through which they view the world might influence and impact their relationships with community organizations.

*Reading and/or Viewing Texts.* Mirra's (2018) framework encourages discussion and empathy throughout engagement with texts. This semester Lucy will be using Wilkerson's (2020) *Caste* and Kaba's (2021) *We Do This 'Til We Free Us* in her CSL courses. These texts are meant to encourage critical thought around socioeconomic class and prison abolition. She has previously used the film *Waiting for "Superman"* (Guggenheim, 2010), to develop thinking about schooling and class. She uses reflective journaling activities that encourage students to make personal connections with the texts and then find additional connections between the text and issues they notice in their communities.

Heather has recently used the documentaries *Intelligent Lives* (Habib, 2018) and *I Learn America* (Dissard & Peng, 2013) to challenge student perspectives on ability, immigration issues, and language proficiency. As they view the documentaries, students complete documentary analysis worksheets in order to guide their reflections on how their perspectives on the groups presented in the videos may have changed or been reinforced.

## Grappling With Privilege

Activities like the ones detailed above are sure to raise complex feelings and thinking from students; on one hand, students may have trauma to cope with from their own experiences with aggressions and microaggressions. On the other hand, some students may struggle to understand what privilege means for them, how they have benefitted from inequity, and how to process all this historical and current complexity. As faculty, we must be prepared to engage with all students.

The key work of establishing safety in the classroom setting must be front-loaded before conversations between faculty and students, students and students, and community partners and students will be possible. Safety is established in the language of syllabi; Lucy includes a statement about Black lives mattering and trans rights being human rights in her syllabus, for example. Safety is also established in the early community building, introductory activities in the class, and it is important for faculty to take the lead in establishing ground rules and encouraging students to develop their own vocabulary around boundaries and expectations for community members. Lucy finds practices from nonviolent communication (Rosenberg, 2015) useful in helping students understand both their own needs and the needs of others.

### Community Connections and Learning

One lesson CSL students must learn is that writing is not an individual, expressivist process, during which they simply find what it is inside of themselves and expel it outwards. Writing is a social process in which writers engage with and are in conversation with people, history, institutions, and culture. Similarly, learning is not an individual, lonely process. Learning happens in conversation with the world. One of the goals of CSL is to encourage teachers and students to be in dialogue with communities, including both on-campus and off-campus entities.

**On-Campus Communities.** Because of CSL coursework, Lucy finds herself and her students interfacing with campus communities more and more frequently. At the small private liberal arts minority-serving university, these organizations and communities include the counseling center, campus ministries, a variety of clubs and student organizations, athletic teams, and campus administration.

Similarly, at the large public university, Heather invites members of the administration, counseling services, Center for Academic Excellence, library, and outdoor adventure offices to provide students with the opportunity to talk to people who provide diverse perspectives. Furthermore, she welcomes members of student organizations to present how they serve the needs of the greater community through their on-campus clubs and programs.

*Off-Campus Communities.* A challenge and an opportunity for CSL faculty are finding ways to include community partners in the work of the course without burdening people who already have a lot on their plates. Inviting community partners to participate in readings and reflections creates an opportunity for people who want to engage with and participate in these kinds of conversations. Additionally, CSL timelines need to be sure to attend to community timelines more than college timelines, which can so easily take precedence in planning. We recommend that these invitations extend beyond the academic semester and that community partners are invited to planning sessions and advisory meetings that occur during the summer and prior to the academic year. These opportunities to influence the direction of the courses prior to the curriculum development for the semester center the needs of the community partners.

### Relational Connections to Content

Freire (1970) describes a transmission theory of education in which information is transmitted to students who accept that information; he then offers critical pedagogy and inquiry-based methods as an alternative to this type of teaching and learning. These are relational pedagogies that "choose a dialogic, relational approach in which our students' knowledge and experience are immediately important and brought directly into the curriculum through ongoing opportunities for personal and social dialogue" (Lysaker & Furuness, 2011, p. 186).

Relational approaches to content include (a) facilitation of community building, (b) fostering a justice-oriented mindset, and (c) building empathy by breaking down stereotype threats. Some practices that facilitate these sorts of relational approaches to content in CSL-driven courses include inquiry groups, relational research, and community writing and presentations.

*Inquiry Groups.* Lucy's process includes encouraging students to develop their own inquiry questions, then forming inquiry groups based on common interests and themes. For example, in a recent semester, the class focused on food and housing instability. Several students had questions around children and food and housing instability, so they formed an inquiry group to track their questions, create a shared informal annotated bibliography, and share their insights and responses once they began working in a community.

Similarly, Heather encourages students to select their community partners based on their own interests; inquiry groups for the legacy projects grow organically out of these partnerships. An example of self-selected partnerships includes preservice teachers often choosing to work with a school-based organization and business and communications majors focusing their efforts on building partnerships with larger community nonprofits that serve the greater community (i.e., Crisis Assistance Ministry).

*Relational Research.* Once students are engaged in CSL work and projects, we encourage them to do secondary research on institutions and work being done in communities, but we also encourage them to learn about such institutions and work relationally. How do community partners feel about what is happening and what needs to happen? This kind of research involves active listening without the need to respond or produce answers.

*Community Writing and Presentations.* CSL is not just for academics; it makes sense, then, that those traditional academic activities, like writing and presentations, be conducted not for an academic audience but for a community audience. Lucy's students have created reports and presentations for community partners, like homeless shelters, and for local school boards, among other audiences. Involving community partners in these activities, when it benefits them to be involved, can also be transformative.

### Shaping a CSL-Driven Syllabus

Creating a syllabus that establishes CSL as a core pedagogy of the course is an important step; the syllabus will set the tone and expectations of the course for students and also holds institutional weight. Barnes et al. (in press) conducted an analysis of CSL syllabi and course materials to consider student positionality. Their findings suggest several areas for faculty writing such syllabi to consider, including the synthesis of CSL core concepts into course documents, the construction of student identity, and the juxtaposition of students with CSL projects and work.

*Weave Concepts Into Course Materials*

The focus on critical consciousness in the course materials reviewed by Barnes et al. (in press) was observable in course documents, including the syllabus, a course contract, and assignments completed for the course.

*Be Thoughtful About Construing Students as Insiders or Outsiders*

Although there may be a tendency to think about students and faculty as generally outsiders to communities being partnered with for SL work, this is often not the case, or, at least, not the whole picture. At the large public university where both Heather and Lucy have taught, some students attending the university went to high school in neighboring communities; these students may consider themselves to be part of their communities still. In Lucy's work with community college students, she has noted that many students consider themselves a part of the communities being partnered with. Additionally, insider and outsider status come, not just from experience with communities but with racial, gender, and ethnic identification as well.

*Consider How to Construe Students With CSL Work*

Barnes et al. (in press) find two major ways in which students were construed: as explorers and as change agents. Exploration, although important, can be problematic, bringing with it the baggage of colonization. Exploration also invokes a sort of focus on the student only, while change agent offers a sense of agency to students and suggests a focus on social justice and the needs of the community.

These three concepts can help with crafting a syllabus and other course materials that situate the course as a CSL course and offer spaces for students that match our pedagogical aims as CSL instructors. In addition to using a syllabus, Heather has used a course contract to encourage that active engagement on the part of students.

*Learning Outcomes and CSL*

In teaching courses with explicit CSL foci, the alignment between the coursework and learning outcomes comes easily. For courses in the disciplines, considering the alignment between learning outcomes and CSL is helpful. In this section, we review learning outcomes from two courses: a first-year composition course and a teacher education methods course. These examples can demonstrate how to align institutional learning outcomes with the work of CSL.

There are often a number of learning outcomes associated with composition courses, so we pull a few of them for this example. These come from the common learning outcomes at a 4-year university, but we have selected outcomes that are common to composition courses:

- Practice and understand writing as a process
- Think critically as writers and work to develop and express your own views and ideas through writing
- Learn to write for a specific audience
- Use writing to extend and deepen your own learning through writing informally, formally, and communicating your learning through writing

As we consider work for the semester that will address these learning goals, since we are applying a CSL perspective, we also want to think about how we can integrate CSL with those learning goals. For the first outcome related to the writing process, we immediately think about how reflections and informal writing in the course can be recursive throughout the semester, ideas and writings students might return to and revise based on their experiences and conversations. We can plan for students to take their initial course reflections and revise them based on their experiences in the course toward the end of the semester. This strategy has the benefit of addressing a problem with revision; students often see revision as an editing process during which comma splices are corrected. Revision is really more about ideas and reimagining a text, so the idea of revising based on additional experience will also help writing students better understand the revision process.

For the second learning outcome about critical thinking, CSL offers clear opportunities. In CSL, we ask ourselves and our students to consider individual backgrounds and perspectives but then to listen and learn from others. This engagement with texts and communities and the problem posing we will do as a part of the reflective process (see Chapter 6 for details on this) encourages critical thinking.

The outcome of learning to write for particular audiences can be met by encouraging students to compose texts that will meet the needs of community partners. These might include texts specifically for community partners but may also include texts advocating for community partners. For example, some of Lucy's students are writing to incarcerated folks as a part of a prison outreach and reform project. These letters are composed to very specific audiences and respond to specific needs. Another of Lucy's students prepared a presentation for a local school board to advocate for a marginalized community within that school, an activity that involved learning how to get on the school board agenda and preparing a text for a particular timeframe and group of people.

The learning outcome about writing to learn will be met by the series of written reflections completed over the course of the semester, which we will describe in greater detail in Chapter 6. Note that because the course we are planning here is a writing course, we might plan for more of the reflections to have written components than we would in other contexts. Our work will be aligning these outcomes with the goals of CSL.

Next, we apply this same process to aligning learning outcomes with CSL goals in a content-oriented course, in this case teacher education. There are also a number of learning outcomes associated with teacher education courses (which are generally aligned with state accreditation processes for teachers). Here we focus on these outcomes, which are fairly general and applied in a variety of teacher education coursework:

- Compare and contrast the purposes and results of formal and informal assessment
- Define, identify, and use in lessons informal classroom assessments, portfolios, performance tasks, projects, presentations, and checklists
- Write lesson plans that meet the specific state guidelines for lesson planning

The task of aligning these course goals with CSL looks a bit different from the writing course, so our process of alignment will look a bit different as well. We first consider community partners and projects that would make sense for this course and these goals. Since we are operating in teacher education, a P–12 partner school or schools might be best. Of course, there are a variety of other options here, including nonprofit programs. Heather and Lucy are associated with the National Writing Project, which means they have a network of local P–12 teachers who are often interested in partnerships. Our initial partnership idea might involve teacher candidates working with small groups selected by classroom teachers over the course of the semester.

For the first learning outcome about understanding the differences between formal and informal assessment, teacher candidates might work with their small group of students on their own learning goals in order to test out their theories and learning about assessment. They might also check in with the P–12 students about assessment practices and their impact on them. Similarly, for the second learning goal about applying assessments, the teacher candidates could create and apply assessment strategies with their small group. As a result of their learning about assessment methods and interacting with P–12 students and teachers, teacher candidates will be more prepared to enter conversations about assessment, labeling, grades, and testing, issues that are directly related to social justice, especially regarding race and class. We might consider reading Wiggan's (2007) "Race, School Achievement, and Educational Inequality: Toward a Student-Based Inquiry Perspective" to facilitate further thought and learning along these lines. Discussions of and responses to this article could include teacher candidates, P–12 teachers, and P–12 high school students.

For the third learning outcome about lesson planning, teacher candidates could continue working with their small group to develop lesson plans. Faculty might encourage the teacher candidates to apply their own understandings about relational learning and social justice to their lesson plans. As these lessons are assessed according to the state guidelines, teacher candidates, faculty, P–12 teachers, and P–12 students could engage in conversations about the constraints and allowances of those state guidelines. What is lost, and what is gained? Who benefits from these guidelines?

In addition to facilitating deep learning around these learning goals, CSL faculty are encouraging community engagement and the enactment of democratic principles, even in situations in which those principles are sometimes sidelined. All of that is part of the work of CSL.

## Conclusion

This chapter has primarily focused on planning for CSL, from activities through the syllabus. In the next chapter, we consider how to facilitate critical reflection throughout the semester and CSL work. The planning pieces managed by faculty will allow them to be fully engaged in the moment once the course and project work commences.

## References

Barnes, M., Steele, L., & Coffey, H. (In press). Focusing on faculty reflection: how university students are positioned in service-learning courses. *Journal of Community Engagement and Higher Education.*

Dissard, J. M., & Peng, G. (2013). *I learn America.* I Learn America.

Freire, P. (1970). *Pedagogy of the oppressed.* Seabury Press.

Gergen, K. J. (2009). *Relational being: beyond self and community.* Oxford University Press.

Guggenheim, D. (Director). (2010). *Waiting for "Superman"* [Film]. Walden Media and Participant Media.

Habib, D. (2018). *Intelligent lives.* Like Right Now Films.

Halberstam, J. (2011). *The queer art of failure.* Duke University Press.

Kaba, M. (2021). *We do this 'til we free us.* Haymarket Books.

Lysaker, J., & Furuness, S. (2011). Space for transformation. *Journal of Transformative Education, 9*(3), 183–197. https://doi.org/10.1177/1541344612439939

McIntosh, P. (1989). White privilege: Unpacking the invisible knapsack. *Peace and Freedom Magazine,* July/August 1989, pp. 10–12.

Mirra, N. (2018). *Educating for empathy: Literacy learning and civic engagement.* Teachers College Press.

Rosenberg, M. (2015). *Nonviolent communication: a language of life: Life-changing tools for healthy relationships* (3rd ed.). PuddleDancer Press.

Teacher Professional Development Group Science Museum of Minnesota. (2015). *Interactive identity wheel.*

Wiggan, G. (2007). Race, school, achievement, and educational inequality: Toward a student-based inquiry perspective. *Review of Educational Research, 77*(3), 310–333. https://doi.org/10.3102/003465430303947

Wilkerson, I. (2020). *Caste: The origins of our discontents.* Random House.

# SIX

# ⁓ Implementing Critical Service-Learning Through Reflective Cycles

"I F YOU'RE COMING OVER TO help me, don't bother. But if you're coming over because you think your liberation is bound up with mine, let's work together" (Weah & Wegner, 1997, p. 211). The development of authentic partnerships among faculty, students, and community partners is incredibly difficult and challenging work, even when everyone is thoroughly invested and engaged; all the stakeholders have complex positions and often different priorities. Honoring and valuing the funds of knowledge, the ideas, and ways of being (Moll et al., 1992), of communities is the way forward for liberatory pedagogies. The quote used to open this paragraph is also the logical endpoint; an Australian Aboriginal woman provided this reflection to researchers Weah and Wegner (1997, p. 211). An attitude of charity toward marginalized communities will do much more harm than good, but keeping focused on the idea that our liberations are all bound up together may create space and opportunity. It is only through a thoughtful plan for reflection that these partnerships can become possible.

In this chapter, we describe the three time-bound spaces for critical reflection and describe the ways in which community partners, students, and faculty can engage in reflection as a dialogic practice before the semester/critical service-learning (CSL) projects begin, during the semester/CSL projects, and at the end of the semester/as CSL projects continue in a new phrase. We also discuss the necessity for these cycles to become recursive.

## Preliminary Reflective Cycles

Before beginning a semester or implementing CSL, engaging in preliminary reflective cycles are crucial for faculty and community partners. Eventually, once CSL projects are off the ground, students will be included in these preliminary reflective cycles; see the Recursive Cycles section for more detailed ideas about including CSL students in these preliminary cycles.

Considering the core idea that developing authentic relationships is an element of CSL (Mitchell, 2008), a structured approach to reflective cycles is a way to encourage empathy and understanding between the people engaging in the projects.

As faculty enter CSL semesters, developing an inquiry stance through reflection will help to model this approach to reflections with students. Faculty might consider the reflective "moves" on the chart below as they develop reflections early in the semester. (See Table 6.1.)

**Table 6.1.** Reflective Moves in Critical Service-Learning

| Move | Key Questions or Prompts | Time Frame |
|---|---|---|
| Inquiry | What questions do you hope to answer through your work this semester? (Note: questions might be around social justice, your field of study, or pedagogy, but they should be your real questions, not model questions, for students to consider. What do you really want to learn through this work?) | Throughout the semester |
| Background and prior experiences | What are the stories that inform your experience with this course, this project, and this community? Who are you, and how does your background impact your position in the classroom? | Preliminary, although these stories will be returned to throughout the work |
| Reactions | What's happening with the project or in the classroom? How are you feeling about what's happening? What do you want or hope for next? | During critical service-learning projects |
| Connections to readings | How do readings connect with what's happening in the classroom and in the field? What are other people's reactions to the readings, and how do they relate to your own responses and connections? | During critical service-learning and at the end of the semester |
| Connections to stakeholders | How have all the components of this experience furthered your understanding? What have you been taught? What skills have you developed as a result of your interactions with stakeholders? | During critical service-learning and at the end of the semester |

Centering O'Grady and Chappell's (2000) concept of *shared control*, which "embodies a commitment to work with, not for, culturally diverse and low-income communities as an alliance of interests" (Boyle-Baise, 2002, p. 13) resonates as we consider reflective cycles as well as the "work" of CSL projects.

Rather than being focused only on the learner, shared control would mean a dual focus, a partnership between the learner and the community. The guiding principles of "reciprocity, mutuality, and empowerment" (Boyle-Baise, 2002, p. 90) should be at the forefront of student activism and community-centered learning.

For faculty facilitating CSL at their institutions and in their classrooms, this shared control must mean including community partners and potential community partners in the preliminary reflective cycle. In this cycle, we recommend asking, "What are the goals of the individuals and organizations with whom we partner?" "What do they see as areas of community abundance and scarcity?" and "What are their questions and concerns?" Including community partners in these initial phases of reflection might be either written or oral, but it's crucial that this inclusion happens as a part of a transparent conversation that either already includes students or will include students once the semester is in progress.

## Developing Critical Reflective Cycles

In their 1996 article, Kahne and Westheimer, having conducted a study of service-learning projects in K–12 classrooms, propose two orientations that apply to service-learning educators: charity and change. Educators interested in charity focus on concepts like altruism and moral development. Educators interested in change focus on concepts like transformation and activism. Table 6.2 demonstrates the service goals for each of the two orientations Kahne and Westheimer describe.

**Table 6.2.** Charity Versus Change Orientations to Service-Learning

| Service-Learning Goals | | | |
|---|---|---|---|
| | *Moral* | *Political* | *Intellectual* |
| *Charity* | Giving | Civic duty | Additive experience |
| *Change* | Caring | Social reconstruction | Transformative experience |

*Source:* Kahne and Westheimer (1996, p. 595, Table 1).

To develop their discussion on this topic, Kahne and Westheimer (1996) analyze reflection, which is a component of almost all service-learning. They point out that reflection can easily result in the calcification of stereotypes and previously held beliefs; citing Richard Paul's work on critical thinking, Kahne and Westheimer (1996) contend that in order to create a transformative educational experience, critical reflection is necessary: "To be critical thinkers, students must be able to consider arguments that justify conclusions that conflict with their own predispositions and self-interest" (p. 598). Mitchell (2008) continues this connection between a critical perspective and reflection:

> Critical service-learning pedagogy fosters a critical consciousness, allowing students to combine action and reflection in classroom and community to examine both the historical precedents of the social problems addressed in their service placements and the impact of their personal action/inaction in maintaining and transforming those problems. This analysis allows students to connect their own lives to the lives of those with whom they work in their service experiences. (p. 54)

Mitchell (2008) further contends that the flow between action and reflection is a part of the praxis of CSL and the move toward social justice.

If it's clear to most CSL educators that a critical approach to reflection is necessary, it may be less clear how to facilitate critical reflection. Next, we look at some examples of reflection from service-learning projects and consider the allowances and constraints of these reflections before moving into practical ways to encourage critical reflection.

### Dangerous Moves in Traditional Service-Learning Reflective Cycles

For Joan Schine (1997), the development of civic-minded youth is an inarguable component of service-learning: "Few people question the propriety of imbuing students with a sense of responsibility and a desire to contribute to the society" (pp. vii–viii). Schine paints a portrait of the past in which children were involved in the activities of the adults in their households and were informal apprentice learners. She points to the service-learning often incorporated in religious educational institutions as a model for service-learning in public schools. This kind of reference indicates the moral ideology that motivates Schine as a service-learning advocate. For her, service-learning in modern schools is a way to encourage these traditional values: "School-based service learning can, to some extent, compensate for the disappearance of those naturally occurring opportunities" (Schine, 1997, p. vii). Schine's (1999) description of a successful service-learning program underscores the moral characteristics she values in adolescents: "They also learn about themselves and others—their strengths and weaknesses, their interests, qualities of leadership, and more. . . . Their budding altruism and their indignation over perceived injustice find an outlet in positive action" (p. 16). There is an interesting tension in Schine's (1999) description. Clearly, the students are meant to gain something abstract and intangible from the process of engaging in service-learning, yet the work should be "altruistic." Schine's (1999) suggestion that service should spark "indignation over perceived injustice" (p. 16) indicates a particular type of student as the subject of service-learning.

This traditional narrative about service-learning depends on a story about the downfall of culture and education, that education and culture today are "worse" than they were at a generally undefined previous time. Schine's perspectives on service-learning point to a previous time when families provided more opportunities for community engagement for their children. Similarly, in his chapter "Youth Participation: Integrating Youth into Communities," Peter Kleinbard (1997), finds that "limited interaction with adults other than teachers has reduced informal educational opportunities for young people" (p. 4) and that "another consequence of the separation of youths and adults is the adults' loss of control of socializing resources" (p. 5). These "deficits" can then be addressed by service-learning. In public education, arguments that depend on this "downfall of culture and family" fallacy are particularly dangerous. The periods of time that such narratives tend to romanticize are generally periods that did not include public education, among other democratic rights, for anyone except for White male students. When this deficit thinking is updated to include high needs schools and students today, these schools and students are either perceived as the recipients of service and giving or as students and sites who require inculcation into the charitable habits and mindsets of the White middle class.

As an example of the kind of reflection that can occur in these charity versions of service-learning, in her chapter "Service Learning in the Classroom: Practical Issues," Winifred Pardo (1997), who founded a service-learning program at a predominantly White, middle-class school in New York, describes the effects of that program. She documents a reflection from an eighth-grade student who participated in the service-learning program and then wrote a letter to the Board of Education. This is an excerpt: "Without Community Service many of the people we help would have nothing. Sometimes we are the only friends or family they have. I just want to say thanks" (Pardo, 1997, pp. 104). An examination of this participant's words reveals a "salvation" narrative in which the objects of the community service are described as having "nothing" without the intervention of the community service students, the subjects of this activity. When the charitable aims of service-learning result in the continued stereotyping of groups of people and perpetuation of the status quo, then we can no longer classify service-learning as a pedagogy with democratic aims. In this style of service-learning, only the privileged learners gain something, and even that gain is suspect.

## Change-Oriented Reflection in CSL

In contrast, Jeff Claus and Curtis Ogden (1999) are service-learning advocates oriented toward change. In their chapter "Service Learning for Youth Empowerment and Social Change: An Introduction," they lay out the case for service-learning and social change: "We like to think that service learning can provide powerful opportunities for youth to reflect critically and constructively on their world and to develop skills for facilitating meaningful social change" (p. 3). Similarly, Maloy et. al. (1999) describe a service-learning project implemented through a partnership between a university and a school district. In this chapter, the authors specifically address the move from student leadership to activism: "Students explored self-chosen issues of social justice and personal identity formation, exercised their voice in group decision making, expressed their ideas to external audiences through publications and performances, and worked for change in school and neighborhood communities" (Maloy et al., 1999, p. 155). This chapter also points out the ways that activism can conflict with traditional schooling, framed from a pedagogical perspective: "Letting students set forth their own concerns and agendas for change also means letting them question and critique why those concerns and agendas are not always addressed within the regular school day" (Maloy et al., 1999, p. 164); Butin (2015) later affirms that CSL often conflicts with the structures of schooling.

In their chapter "Promoting Identity Development: Ten Ideas for School-Based Service-Learning Programs," Miranda Yates and James Youniss (1999) provide examples of reflections from students engaged in service-learning at a predominantly Black-, middle-, and lower class school in a major northeastern city. This parochial school's involvement in service-learning comes from a charity orientation with a significant focus on giving. Yates and Youniss (1999) document this student reflection:

> There was a man [at the soup kitchen]. I didn't catch his name but he had an obvious mental problem, and my classmates and I laughed at him for a few minutes. Then I realized that he was going to be like that forever. There was no one to help him and probably no one who cared. It hurt to realize that I was sitting among society's forgotten. The people I read about every day at school and in the newspapers. I wanted to cry, but I didn't, I couldn't, they didn't need my pity. They needed my action. (pp. 52)

Clearly, this project and the nature of the reflection differed tremendously from the project and the type of reflection completed in Pardo's article. The type of reflection produced by the service-learning participant is markedly different, which indicates that a more critical reflection component was requested. Also, however, the identities, races, and socioeconomic backgrounds of the student participants were different. Lisa Delpit (1995) points to the type of listening and engagement that yields this type of critical reflection: "We must learn to be vulnerable enough to allow our world to turn upside down in order to allow the realities of others to edge themselves into our consciousness" (p. 47). Service-learning that encourages students to engage in this kind of vulnerability will look quite different from service-learning meant to calcify a current belief system.

*Radical Vulnerability Through Reflection*

In many service-learning projects, participants are asked to produce critical reflections, but researchers have noticed that such reflections are as likely to reinforce stereotypes and understandings of privilege as they are to disrupt them. Considering ways to elicit critical reflections from everyone involved, from faculty, students, community members, and other stakeholders is an area of growth and research for proponents of experiential learning, and especially in teacher education programs in which we teach. Although he is speaking to the field of education, Emdin's (2016) perspective on the necessary vulnerability for White teachers is relevant for all CSL faculty, particularly White teachers: "The work for white folks who teach in urban schools, then, is to unpack their privileges and excavate the institutional, societal, and personal histories they bring with them when they come to the hood" (p. 15).

What does critical reflection look like in a CSL classroom then? Reflection will include a few key metrics:

- Reflection is ongoing, not only an end-of-the-semester activity.
- Faculty and students participate in reflection, and there are opportunities for community partners to participate as well.
- Reflection is a part of a dialogic process, not only an internalized, individual process.
- Reflection encourages radical vulnerability on the parts of all participants.

Faculty facilitating CSL reflection might consider ways in which reflection can be dialogic. Although a faculty member commenting on a written student reflection can be dialogic, especially if there are ways for students to speak back, there are also a variety of other ways to encourage reflection as a part of the work and conversation of the course. Here are a few suggestions.

*Dialogic Journals.* This type of reflection can take a number of forms. One method Lucy often uses is a four-column or -box strategy, which can also work on an online discussion board. The first entry includes either a quote (from a text, student, faculty member, or community partner) or an incident. The second entry is the reflecter's reaction or response to the catalyst quote or incident. The third entry is a response from someone else; the someone else could be a student, faculty, or community partner. The fourth entry is the original writer's return to the topic after the conversation. For more details on how to adapt this sort of strategy, we recommend *Thinking Out Loud on Paper: The Student Daybook as a Tool to Foster Student Learning* (Brannon et al., 2008).

*Discussions.* Discussions can be whole class, small groups, partners, or beyond the classroom, including community partners or other interested stakeholders. These conversations can be live events in person or via electronic services, or they might happen asynchronously online. One benefit to discussions is that they encourage active listening and thinking.

*Text Sets.* One way to support discussions is through the inclusion of text sets. We build on our work with the National Writing Project's College, Career, and Community Writing Program (C3WP), which guides writers in developing arguments through selecting and organizing evidence in order to engage in civic discourse. Using or building collections of texts that represent a variety of viewpoints on selected topics, instructors (and students) make claims in their development of an argument and use information from texts that support these arguments. So how do text sets and arguments support the goals of CSL? By challenging students to remove emotion from a discussion about a controversial topic through the use of evidence on both sides of the topic, they are able to reflect on how their perspectives are informed by facts or evidence. This way of reflecting on evidence makes challenging their own preconceived notions of diverse groups part of their everyday assessment of the world.

*Annotated Reflections.* This strategy initially looks like a traditional written reflection completed by a CSL participant. These annotated reflections should be living texts, which allow people commenting privileges on the document. This can be done using frequently used word processing applications, like Microsoft Word or Google Docs, but might include other annotation tools, like Kami. Comments can be added by students, faculty members, or community partners and should encourage the reflection writer to consider and revise their thinking.

*Community Journaling.* To encourage conversation and discussion among students, faculty, and community partners, dialogic journals can be adapted to include community partners as thinking partners, either in writing or verbally. Additionally, faculty should be prepared to innovate to address the needs of community partners. Using art or digital tools may meet the needs of community partners more aptly than written journals, so it's crucial for faculty to stay attuned. Another strategy might be improvisation games; if there is tension around a topic or issue, a *rant* is helpful. To do a rant, everyone stands in a circle and then faces away from the group. Anyone who wants to speak or rant turns back to face the center of the circle until another participant turns around to speak. Then, the speaker stops talking and turns back around. This activity proceeds as long as it is helpful. For a deeper dive into the theory behind improvisation and disrupting power relationships, Ryan Welsh's (2014) dissertation "On Improvisation, Learning and Literacy" is helpful. For practical educational resources, see "Improvisation in teaching and education—roots and applications" by Holdhus et al. (2016).

## Concluding the Semester/Continuing CSL

The end of the semester brings a certain tension for CSL participants. Semesters necessarily end; grades are due, students move out of their dorms, and college life enters one of the periods of lull that characterize the pattern of 4-year college life and work. CSL projects, however, often cannot and do not live and breathe in the same patterns as college semesters. Butin (2015) notes that projects may be completed much earlier than the semester, but in many cases, those projects will continue long past the deadlines associated with any given course.

Both Heather and Lucy use end-of-the-semester reflections and/or portfolios as ways to assess CSL coursework, but these methods of assessment pose certain dangers to critical analysis. As a longtime college composition instructor, Lucy can attest to the tendency of students and faculty to tell certain types of stories about their experiences; often these stories tell of obstacles encountered and overcome, journeys completed. These kinds of stories have a certain finished quality: the work is done; the student is complete (or graduated or equipped with the skills the course was offering). Our work in shifting power dynamics and moving toward greater justice will not be complete at the end of the semester, so it's crucial for us to help students craft narratives that suggest that unfinished quality in their reflections. It's also useful for faculty and community partners to embrace that ellipsis, instead of a period, at the end of the semester (see Chapter 4 for a more detailed description).

### Recursive Cycles

CSL projects often continue, even when the course or the college semester is complete. It makes sense then that the reflective cycles for CSL projects might not align directly with the flow of the semester. While there will often be certain kinds of preliminary reflections for students beginning their engagement with CSL at the beginning of the semester, the in-progress flow for reflections will depend on the flow of the project and the needs of the community partners, faculty, and students involved. Even end-of-the-semester reflections may serve different roles or purposes, depending on the nature of the work and the ways in which stakeholders have engaged with it. One end-of-the-semester question Lucy likes to pose is, What's next? This might be an invitation for students and community partners to consider their personal next steps, or it may be an invitation for reflections to consider what's next for the project itself, which may or not be complete in any meaningful ways. One of the keys to facilitating critical reflection is to be in the moment and aware of what kinds of conversations need to be happening at that moment in time.

There are also ways to keep stakeholders involved in projects and reflections beyond the confines of the college semester. At some institutions, course shells can continue to be in use even when the semester is done. There is also the potential to use email or other online spaces to continue the crucial conversations that begin during CSL experiences. Furthermore, CSL students might continue to work with the community partner in a volunteer capacity once the semester has ended. We discuss these recursive moves and provide discussion and reflection prompts in the workbook that aligns with this text.

## References

Boyle-Baise, M. (2002). *Multicultural service learning: educating teachers in diverse communities.* Teachers College Press.

Brannon, L., Griffin, S., Haag, K., Iannone, A., Urbanski, C., & Woodward, S. (2008). *Thinking out loud on paper: The student daybook as a way to foster student learning.* Heinemann.

Butin, D. (2015). Dreaming of justice: Critical service-learning and the need to wake up. *Theory into Practice, 54*(1), 5–10. https://doi.org/10.1080/00405841.2015.977646

Claus, J., & Ogden, O. (1999), *Service learning for youth empowerment and social change.* Peter Lang.

Delpit, L. (1995). *Other people's children: cultural conflict in the classroom.* The New Press.

Emdin, C. (2016). *For White folks who teach in the hood . . . and the rest of y'all too: Reality pedagogy and urban education.* Beacon Press.

Holdhus, K., Høisæter, S., Mæland, K., Vangsnes, V., Engelsen, K. S., Espeland, M., & Espeland, A. (2016). Improvisation in teaching and education—roots and applications. *Cogent Education, 3*(1). https://doi.org/10.1080/2331186X.2016.1204142

Kahne, J., & Westheimer, J. (1996, May). In the service of what? The politics of service learning. *The Phi Delta Kappan, 77*(9), 592–599. https://www.jstor.org/stable/20405655

Kleinbard, P. (1997). Youth participation: integrating youth into communities. In J. Schine (Ed.), *Service learning: Ninety-sixth yearbook of the national society for the study of education, part I* (pp. 1–18). University of Chicago Press.

Maloy, R. W., Sheehan, A. S., LaRoche, I. S., & Clark, R. J. (1999). Building legacies: school improvement and youth activism in an urban teacher education partnership. In J. Claus & C. Ogden (Eds.), *Service learning for youth empowerment and social change* (pp. 143–167). Peter Lang.

Mitchell, T. D. (2008, Spring). Traditional vs. critical service-learning: Engaging the literature to differentiate two models. *Michigan Journal of Community Service-Learning, 14*(2), 50–65. http://hdl.handle.net/2027/spo.3239521.0014.205

Moll, L. C., Amanti, C., Neff, D., & Gonzalez, N. (1992). Funds of knowledge for teaching using a qualitative approach to connect homes and classrooms. *Theory Into Practice, 31*(2), 132–141. https://www.jstor.org/stable/i264774

O'Grady, C. R., & Chapell, B. (2000). With, not for: The politics of service learning in multicultural communities. In C. J. Ovando & P. McLaren (Eds.), *The politics of multiculturalism and bilingual education: Students and teachers caught in the crossfire* (pp. 209–224). McGraw Hill.

Pardo, W. (1997). Service-learning in higher education. In J. Schine (Ed.), *Service-learning* (pp. 90–104). NSSE.

Schine, J. (1997). Editor's preface. In *Service learning: ninety-sixth yearbook of the national society for the study of education, part I.* (pp. vii–ix.) University of Chicago Press.

Schine, J. (1999). Beyond test scores and standards: Service, understanding, and citizenship. In J. Claus & C. Ogden (Eds.), *Service learning for youth empowerment and social change* (pp. 9–24). Peter Lang.

Weah, W., & Wegner, M. (1997). A catalyst for social action and school change at the middle level. In S. Totten & J. E. Pedersen (Eds.), *Social issues and service at the middle level* (pp. 211–233). Allyn and Bacon.

Welsh, R. C. (2014). *On improvisation, learning, and literacy* (Publication No. 3636175) [Doctoral dissertation, University of North Carolina at Charlotte]. ProQuest Dissertations Publishing.

Yates, M., & Youniss, J. (1999). Promoting identity development: Ten ideas for school-based service-learning programs. In J. Claus & C. Ogden (Eds.) *Service learning for youth empowerment and social change* (pp. 43–67). Peter Lang.

# SEVEN

# ❧ Faculty Development for Critical Service-Learning

A S WE WRITE THIS CHAPTER, Heather's campus is considering minor changes in its service-learning designation; the new goal would be to incorporate a focus on critical service-learning (CSL). As such, there will be a need for faculty development in the area of CSL, which has given us pause to think deeply about how we would recommend a college or university develop a plan for this challenge. McKee and Tew (2013) assert that faculty must always be prepared "through ongoing enhancement of their abilities and intellect to answer the call to lead their prospective institutions through the morass of uncertainty brought about by cultural, national, and even worldwide current and future realities" (p. 3). Regardless of topic or skill, effective faculty must engage in development through activities that encourage continual growth in their professional practice to keep up with the trends and research in higher education. When the current political and social landscape is furthering divisive outcomes for the country, we need to seek to heal through building understanding and empathy; this current climate highlights the need for a more critical model of service-learning and faculty development in this area.

Our comprehensive review of literature in the field of faculty development for service-learning revealed many studies focused on the research on the topic, but we did not find any resources or research related to faculty development within the area of CSL. Advancing the call for a wider range of settings to study (i.e., public, private, 4-year, and 2-year; cross-institutional), we offer the following chapter as a model for faculty development at a public 4-year university, a community college, and a four-year private university.

We begin this chapter by building on the work of Welch and Plaxton-Moore (2017) and Berkey et al. (2018), whose work comprehensively describes the most common formats for faculty/professional development in the area of service-learning and community engagement and thoughtfully offers recommendations for building faculty development models. Then, we discuss the varied levels of faculty development in the area of service-learning and civic engagement that we notice in the literature and provide in-depth recommendations for how higher education can support the integration of CSL practices with faculty. Essentially, we seek to demonstrate how faculty development in the area of CSL might be different from and potentially more effective at encouraging a more activist mindset than programs that support faculty in the implementation of traditional service-learning.

## Faculty Development in Service-Learning in Higher Education

Although service-learning is a popular pedagogy for introducing students to civic engagement and scholarship, research suggests that faculty who are intrinsically motivated by volunteerism and service are typically drawn to these types of courses (Stanton, 1994). According to research conducted by Driscoll (2000), those who teach courses with service-learning components are usually faculty within the first 3 years of teaching at the college level or are tenured educators (i.e., associate/full professors) who have already developed a research agenda and have had time to develop community partnerships later in their career. Often, these tenured, more veteran faculty teach at universities with a civic engagement focus. There appears to be a dearth of research that focuses on why certain faculty are attracted to service-learning and the motivations for engaging in this time-consuming pedagogy often not recognized in the tenure and promotion process.

Pribbenow (2005) found that faculty who teach service-learning focused courses reported deeper connections and relationships with students as learners and individuals, enhanced knowledge of student learning processes and outcomes, increased use of constructivist teaching and learning approaches, improved communication of theoretical concepts, and greater involvement in a community of teachers and learners. Similar research suggests that there are multiple factors that both motivate and discourage faculty from taking up a practice of service-learning (Abes et al., 2002; Mundy, 2003). Often, these factors include institutional barriers and time commitments; however, the benefit of engaging students in meaningful and relevant experiences and an gaining understanding of community issues often overshadows the negative.

*Recommendations for Faculty Development for Service-Learning*

Bringle and Hatcher (1995) recommended "a deliberate, organized, and centralized approach to faculty development" (p. 113), which these recommendations and the Critical Service-Learning Implementation Model (CSLIM) address. Like the reflective components of CSL, faculty development components must include preliminary activities, opportunities for reflection and development during the semester, and post-CSL discussion and reflection.

Pribbenow (2005) proposed that faculty development in the area of service-learning must include "reconceptualizing classroom norms and roles, enhancing their understanding of student and community needs, and in some cases, expanding opportunities for their scholarship" (p. 25).

Furthermore, Pribbenow (2005) recognized that there is a need for faculty development through affinity groups and a broad-ranging approach "that encourages faculty reflection and growth within the context of a community or communities of teachers and learners" (p. 35). In order for faculty to fully engage in professional development, Pribbenow recommended that they participate in preparation, meaningful action, reflection, and evaluation and cautioned that faculty might not be as willing to engage in development when there is too much oversight and assessment requirements from university administrators.

***Common Approaches for Faculty Development in Service-Learning.*** In order to find "salient features and trends of existing faculty development programming designed to advance service-learning and community engagement in higher education" (Welch & Plaxton-Moore, 2017, p. 132), Welch and Plaxton-Moore (2017) conducted a comprehensive review of the literature of faculty development programming and conducted a survey about practice and formats of faculty development in the area. According to their research, approximately 70% of respondents from campuses with the Carnegie Classification for Community Engagement reported that they provide faculty development programming. Furthermore, 90% reported offering "one-on-one consultation, technical assistance, and resource materials to support faculty in developing and implementing various forms of engaged teaching and scholarship" (Welch & Plaxton-Moore, 2017, p. 131). More recently, a 2015 survey of Campus Compact members, indicated that a little over 75% of the campuses that responded offer "(a) faculty development workshops/fellowships, (b) materials to assist faculty with reflection and assessment, and (c) curriculum models and sample syllabi" (Welch & Plaxton-Moore, 2017, p. 131).

Welch and Plaxton-Moore (2017) also noted that most faculty development programs usually consist of the following features (ordered from most to least common):

- A series of 1- to 2-hour workshops and onetime half-day workshops
- One-on-one consultations and workshops
- Community partner guest speakers and colleague mentors
- Minimal time commitment for faculty
- Faculty learning communities/affinity groups
- Other formats: symposia, webinars, conferences, faculty fellow seminars
- Format is most commonly conducted on campus during semester or summer
- Mostly attended by new (1–3 years) or tenured faculty with occasional doctoral student participation development

Although there appears to be a trend toward growth in the area of faculty development (Van Note Chism et al., 2013), there is also a commitment to a competency-based approach (Blanchard et al., 2009) that challenges faculty to assimilate and apply new information and skills over time. Blanchard et al. (2009) identified 14 competencies that define an engaged scholar, which include

> understanding and applying the concepts, principles, theory, and practice of community-engaged scholarship; transferring skills to working with partners; disseminating new knowledge gained from community-engaged scholarship through publications and presentations; balancing and integrating community-engaged scholarship within the trilogy of academic missions (teaching, research, and service); and preparation for and successful reward of promotion and tenure. (p. 135)

While Axtell (2012) suggested that general faculty development typically consists of the following foci: (a) skills, (b) career development, (c) critical reflection, (d) building and sustaining relationships, and (e) navigating and changing the institutional system. Holland (1997) suggested that institutions commit to service-learning by defining guidelines for promotion, tenure, and hiring. Gelmon et al. (1998) endorsed "regular and sustained faculty development activities" (p. 268) as a path to progress for service-learning.

*Format.* Through their surveys of institutions of higher education, Welch and Plaxton-Moore (2017) also found that there were a variety of formats for implementation of faculty development in service-learning and community engagement. Six of the most common areas for programming include reflection, course development, principles of community engagement, syllabus development, assessment, and establishing/maintaining community partnerships, all of which are the building blocks to a service-learning practice. Some survey respondents reported a secondary focus on teaching about community-based research and critical pedagogical models, more advanced competencies, which is related to our particular inquiry about faculty development in the area of CSL.

Throughout the literature, there are several theoretical frameworks that inform faculty development in the area of service-learning and community engagement. Freire's (1970) concept of critical pedagogy is a touchstone for CSL, especially considering Mitchell's (2008) elements of authentic relationships and interest in power dynamics. In order to develop faculty in CSL, training activities should model these Freirean ideas and offer faculty participants opportunities to build authentic relationships with each other and develop their own understandings of CSL, as opposed to banking-style faculty development that simply provides information and reasserts classroom power dynamics.

We also draw on Mirra's (2018) theory of critical civic empathy. Mirra defines empathy as the ability to see the world from another person's vantage point. Over the past 5 or so years (since a very polarizing American presidential election in 2016), divisive political and social movements have made it quite clear that our society is desperately lacking empathy. We contend that engaging undergraduate students in CSL has the potential to build empathy necessary to better understand other people's perspectives and experiences; thus, critical civic empathy would be included in any faculty development related to CSL. Despite a focus on secondary literacy teachers, Mirra's work encourages educators to consider how issues of power and inequity happen in classrooms and how to envision literacy practices, such as reflection and discourse act as a means of civic engagement. Mirra (2018) explains that critical civic empathy includes three components:

1. It begins from an analysis of the social position, power, and privilege of all parties involved.
2. It focuses on the way that personal experiences matter in the context of public life.
3. It fosters democratic dialogue and civic action committed to equity and justice. (p. 7)

We argue that CSL and critical civic empathy go hand in hand in a way that may have positive outcomes for those who participate in service-learning courses. In tandem with CSL, a critical approach to empathy encourages us to interrogate what we each bring to the table when we seek to empathize with others and to acknowledge the fact that the ways in which we are privileged (or marginalized) in public life inevitably influence how we interpret the experiences of others (Mirra, 2018, pp. 7–8).

With this in mind, we contend that faculty development in the realm of CSL must support faculty in crafting and addressing questions about the roots of social inequality with their students. As Berkey et al. (2018) suggest, those planning faculty development must move

> beyond being competent workshop facilitator[s] to being transformative leader[s] who provide professional education to faculty, administrators, and community partners about the nature of this work [and who] will influence the trajectory of the institution to embed and advance community engagement within its mission. (p. 29)

*Levels of Service-Learning Support*

As we conceptualize how institutions of higher education might build a strong faculty development program in CSL, we draw on the work of Furco (1999), who identifies five dimensions that characterize the institutionalization of service-learning and the components that characterize each dimension: (1) Philosophy and Mission of Service-Learning, (2) Faculty Support for and Involvement in Service-Learning, (3) Student Support for and Involvement in Service-Learning, (4) Community Participation and Partnerships, and (5) Institutional Support for Service-Learning. Furco cautions that this work, like any other reform, takes time and commitment in order to be effective. In this self-assessment tool, Furco highlights three stages of capacity building—*Critical Mass Building, Quality Building, and Sustained Institutionalization.* We build on these stages in our own vision for institutional development in the area of CSL and categorize the elements based on resources, financial and human support, and time and energy commitment provided by the institution related to faculty development in CSL.

*Critical Mass Building.* We decided that the first stage of engagement in a path to focusing on CSL would include the most common practices found among colleges and universities across the United States. These components do not necessarily require action on the part of the faculty member but rather the university's outward expression of a focus on service-learning and community engagement. These components are predicated upon the institution's commitment to CSL:

- Publication of an institutional statement on critical service-learning and community engagement as part of the mission of the institution
- Assistance with finding community partners committed to transformative social change
- Curriculum development in the form of online resources from courses that promote CSL (i.e., syllabus repository; publications; toolkits/ workbooks)
- Funding for CSL faculty to attend conferences such as PACE (Pathways to Achieving Civic Engagement), IARSLCE (International Association for Research in Service-Learning and Civic Engagement), AERA (American Education Research Association), NYLC (National Youth Leadership Conference), and Campus Compact to gain valuable tools and learn about research related to CSL
- Programmatic website with programs/courses, awards and funding, community partners, calendar, stories, and opportunities for funding
- Online modules for preparing to plan and teach a CSL course (housed on a website or through a learning management system)
- Course support grants (to fund workshop attendance or community events)

*Quality Building.* At the Quality Building level of faculty development, the campus has to commit time and resources to support active faculty development in CSL, and faculty also has to invest time and effort into growing their practice. This advanced level also requires a deeper investment into the communities surrounding the campus and an understanding of the reciprocal nature of effective CSL. The following are the components of faculty development at this level:

- Official campus office or department; see, for example:
  - APPLES/Carolina Center for Public Service (University of North Carolina at Chapel Hill) https://ccps.unc.edu/apples/
  - Bonner Center for Civic Engagement (University of Richmond) https://engage.richmond.edu/
  - Center for Community-Engaged Learning (University of Minnesota) https://ccel.umn.edu/
- Faculty Fellowship: Member(s) of the faculty presents research findings throughout the academic year related to civic engagement work and supports faculty as they develop their CSL teaching and research agenda.
- Semester symposia focused on faculty and student service-learning projects
- Monthly affinity group meetings for faculty, staff, and community partners to share initiatives and problem pose on issues of concern
- Monthly sessions on building relationships with community partners
- Certification or designation process whereby faculty have clear expectations and institutional support for engaging in a CSL course
- Financial and technical support for creating a research agenda around critical service-learning and community engagement; small grants and mentoring services for creating a research study focused on content
- Professional development around curriculum building with a focus integrating critical pedagogy informed by current policy/events
- Faculty development sessions/modules on positioning students as transformative social change agents; as leaders; at the center of inquiry

*Sustained Institutional Level.* This book centers on crafting a practice in CSL, and as such we recommend building on the quality-building level of faculty development in order to promote understanding and institutional integration of components of CSL. Musil (2009) contends that institutions of higher education are situated in a position not only to promote civic engagement but to also provide a platform to question issues of equity and social justice and to develop the necessary skills to advocate for community-based solutions. As such, professional development in CSL must model for faculty how to engage students in reflection and inquiry in ways that uncover inequitable distributions of power and resources and move them into an activist mindset. Building on the work of Harkins et al. (2020) and Campus Compact (1999), we envision faculty development through the following statement:

> CSL pedagogy addresses these concerns and aims to promote social justice by educating students on how to deconstruct theoretically, empirically, and practically the power structures that underlie many traditional views of the world. (Harkins et al., 2020, p. 22)

Although we did not find specific language in the literature related to CSL, we did find some characteristics of CSL we would define as essential to faculty development in this area. More specifically, we advocate for a train-the-trainer model (we are definitely National Writing Project people), which would put faculty already engaged in a practice of CSL in the role of training others how to transform their pedagogy and curriculum.

## Campuses Advancing the Goals of CSL

We contend that colleges and universities must make a public statement, whether via university website or memorandum related to a nuanced understanding of the difference between traditional and CSL and that they are committed to CSL. Furthermore, universities must acknowledge that CSL requires much more time than a typical course. Not only do faculty need to build a trusting community within the classroom in order to foster deep, critical discussions about potentially sensitive topics related to political, social, and religious, among other, ideologies, they need time to introduce the community partners into the setting so that students understand the collaborative nature of these courses.

In the state where Heather teaches, 4-year state universities were required to change their course meeting format. Before this change, Heather taught a 3-hour course on a Friday morning; she began the semester with the course meeting on campus and continued to meet at the community partner site by the fourth week of the semester. Now, her course is scheduled in the middle of the day for 1 hour 20 minutes on Tuesdays and Thursdays. Prior to the change, her students spent a substantial time both during course time and outside of course time with community partners; however, the schedule change made it impossible for her students to travel off campus to a course sandwiched between two others. The very nature of service-learning courses requires an investment of time outside of the routine of the university schedule; the university that supports CSL must allow for opportunities for these courses to meet outside of the parameter of regularly scheduled course times. This recommendation is supported by Harkins et al. (2020), who write, "Institutional support could include increasing the course credit for service-learning courses for students and providing advanced learning credits, assistantships, stipends, and research opportunities for peer mentors" (p. 31).

In order for a two-or four-year college to demonstrate support of the goals of CSL, there must be an outward commitment to supporting the faculty through communication with the public and a dedication to promoting CSL through granting requests for nontraditional course meeting times and locations.

### CSL Educator Institute

Each year, the NYLC hosts the 2-day Service-Learning Educator Institute, during which K–16 educators seek to better understand how service-learning can "transform their classrooms, schools, and communities" (NYLC, n.d., para. 2). With a focus on constructivist teaching, participants learn about research-based practices for service-learning and build their own units of instruction using a backward design approach (Wiggins et al., 1998). Furthermore, participants developed rigorous activities and assessments aligned with their K–16 curriculum standards all while gaining a deeper understanding of how to include students in the process of planning and implementation of the unit. Typically marketed to a variety of stakeholders in the educational setting, the Service-Learning Educator Institute provides a potential model for how college campuses might build support faculty in their venture into CSL.

Harkins et al's (2020) work informs our vision for a Critical Service-Learning Educator Institute that would include discussion and engagement around (a) providing a social change orientation, (b) working to redistribute power, and (c) developing authentic relationships. This intense 2-day institute would also include coaching on how to engage students in difficult, often un-comfortable conversations while addressing privilege and bias. Although a critical approach to anything at this point requires this kind of orientation, we have attended very few faculty development opportunities that teach us how to discuss these challenging concepts with our students. We recommend that any faculty development workshop that engages with CSL must prepare fac-ulty to support their students as they may deal with difficult realizations about how the inequitable distribution of power and resources has benefited them.

*Peer Mentoring*

We advocate for the creation and support of a peer-mentoring program for CSL courses. Peer mentors can model for students how to challenge their own theoretical and experiential understandings and how they might work with community partners to advocate for change. In her undergraduate ser-vice-learning course, Heather utilized the university's preceptor program to hire a peer mentor who had already engaged in the course. In this role, the peer mentor led class discussions about social justice and equity as well as served as a bridge between community partners and undergraduate students. The peer mentor also worked individually with undergraduates to plan their social justice action project and with small groups on the course's legacy proj-ect (See Appendix II for a description of course assignments). Peer mentoring provides a supportive opportunity for undergraduates to gain the skills nec-essary to more deeply engage with how and why we choose to "help" (Harkins et al., 2017). We contend that by providing faculty with the necessary tools to recruit and train peer mentors for CSL courses, these peer mentors can pro-vide undergraduates with a model of how to engage in critical reflection and participate in discussions that challenge power relations/policies.

Any faculty development that supports peer mentoring should require fac-ulty members and peer mentors to participate in community- and curricu-lum-building activities. We contend that peer mentors should also participate in the planning of a course so that they have a deeper understanding of their role and how the curriculum supports the goals of CSL from the teaching perspective. Peer mentors and faculty members should also learn more about how to ask reflective questions in ways that challenge students to view situa-tions and readings through a more critical lens.

*Faculty Fellowships*

Faculty development in the form of faculty fellowships is an essential support opportunity for those endeavoring to engage in CSL. A faculty fellow ideally would receive a stipend and course release to present workshops and develop modules that focus on developing curriculum and resources. Furthermore, a faculty fellow might work one-on-one with instructors on syllabus creation and seeking out community partnerships. The Bonner Center for Civic Engagement at the University of Virginia offers a model for how 2- and 4-year colleges might set up a faculty fellowship; in addition to a stipend and course release, the faculty fellow might receive additional funding for their own development in the form of conference and workshop attendance. Additional support might also include stipends to support faculty work on syllabi and activities over the summer, ongoing pedagogical support from the campus teaching and learning group, and offsetting the time and travel costs associated with developing relationships with community partners.

*Features of the Classroom*

Harkins et al. (2020) contend that a social change approach to service-learning, like that identified by Mitchell (2008), promote community and campus connections among students and suggest that "students' relationships with their professors, community partners, and peer mentors help facilitate (p. 21) these connections. In their study of 125 undergraduates attending a midsized university in the Northeast, researchers found that more resources and smaller class sizes and the support of peer mentors helped establish and nourish stronger relationships among students, faculty, peer mentors, and community partners. Moreover, we recommend university support for CSL in the form of smaller class sizes, flexible seating in active learning classrooms, integration of campus resources that support community-building and problem-solving activities (i.e., mobile team-building activities).

## Recommendations for Support for New CSL Faculty

As we consider the ways in which colleges and universities can support new faculty who plan to teach CSL courses, we cannot stress enough the importance of combining a research, teaching, and service agenda. There is so much we do not yet know about the ways in which faculty, students, and community partners experience CSL that we recommend campuses engage their new faculty in exploring the potential of this curriculum and pedagogy. More specifically, we recommend that new CSL faculty are assigned mentors who can help them navigate setting up a practice that combines all three components of the tenure and promotion process. This more experienced faculty member might support newer faculty by helping with the integration of CSL components to existing or new syllabi, identifying organizations and projects that connect to course objectives, attending faculty development workshops and individual consultations together, and introducing the new faculty to the greater community/town/city.

*Next Steps for Faculty Development*

There are multiple efficacious models for faculty development in the area of service-learning and community engagement provided by various institutions around the United States. Through our review of the literature, we have learned that institutions of higher education are committed to service-learning and community engagement on a variety of levels. Based on our findings, there exists a need for more detailed plans for faculty development in the area of CSL in order to promote the type of engagement that seeks to transform society into a more equitable environment that exposes the root causes of oppression and marginalization. We hope that our vision for faculty development for CSL provides a model for institutions endeavoring to engage undergraduates and community partners to advocate for community-based solutions.

## References

Abes, E. S., Jackson, G., & Jones, S. R. (2002). Factors that motivate and deter faculty use of service-learning. *Michigan Journal of Community Service Learning, 9*(1), 5–17. http://hdl.handle.net/2027/spo.3239521.0009.101

Axtell, S. (2012). *Creating a community-engaged scholarship (CES) faculty development program—Phase one: Program and skill mapping.* University of Michigan. http://www.engagement.umn.edu/faculty/tools

Berkey, B., Meixner, C., Green, P. M., & Eddins, E. A. (2018). *Reconceptualizing faculty development in service-learning/community engagement: Exploring intersections, frameworks, and models of practice.* Stylus.

Blanchard, L. W., Hanssmann, C., Strauss, R. P., Belliard, J. C., Krichbaum, K., Waters, E., & Seifer, S. D. (2009). Models for faculty development: What does it take to be a community-engaged scholar? *Metropolitan Universities, 20*(2), 47–65.

Bringle, R. G., & Hatcher, J. A. (1995). A service-learning curriculum for faculty. *Michigan Journal of Community Service Learning, 2*, 112–122. http://hdl.handle.net/2027/spo.3239521.0002.111

Campus Compact. (1999). *Presidents' declaration on the civic responsibility of higher education.* https://compact.org/resources-for-presidents/presidents-declaration-on-the-civic-responsibility-of-higher-education/

Driscoll, A. (2000, Fall). Studying faculty and service-learning: Directions for inquiry and development. *Michigan Journal of Community Service Learning: Strategic Directions for Service-Learning Research*, 35–41. http://hdl.handle.net/2027/spo.3239521.spec.105

Freire, P. (1970). *Pedagogy of the oppressed.* Seabury Press.

Furco, A. (1999). *Self-assessment rubric for the institutionalization of service-learning in higher education.* Service-Learning Research and Development Center, University of Berkeley, California.

Gelmon, S. B., Holland, B. A., Shinnamon, A. F., & Morris, B. A. (1998). Community-based education and service: The HPSISN experience. *Journal of Interprofessional Care, 12*(3), 257–272. https://doi.org/10.3109/13561829809014117

Harkins, D., Grenier, L., Irizarry, C., Robinson, E., Ray, S., & Shea, L. (2020). Building relationships for critical service-learning. *Michigan Journal of Community Service Learning, 26*(2), 21–37. https://doi.org/10.3998/mjcsloa.3239521.0026.202

Holland, B. (1997). Analyzing institutional commitment to service. *Michigan Journal of Community Service Learning, 4*(1), 30–41. http://hdl.handle.net/2027/spo.3239521.0004.104

McKee, C., & Tew, W. (2013). Setting the stage for teaching and learning in American higher education: Making the case for faculty development. *New Directions for Teaching and Learning, 2013*(133), 3–14. https://doi.org/10.1002/tl.20041

Mirra, N. (2018). *Educating for empathy: Literacy learning and civic engagement.* Teachers College Press.

Mitchell, T. D. (2008, Spring). Traditional vs. critical service-learning: Engaging the literature to differentiate two models. *Michigan Journal of Community Service-Learning, 14*(2), 50–65. http://hdl.handle.net/2027/spo.3239521.0014.205

Mundy, M. E. (2003). *Faculty engagement in service-learning: Individual & organizational factors at distinct institutional types.* [Unpublished doctoral dissertation]. Vanderbilt University, Nashville.

Musil, C. M. (2009). Educating students for personal and social responsibility: The civic learning spiral. In B. Jacoby (Ed.), *Civic engagement in higher education: Concepts and practices* (pp. 49–68). Jossey-Bass.

National Youth Leadership Council. (n.d.). *Service-Learning Educator Institute.* https://www.nylc.org/page/educator-institute

Pribbenow, D. A. (2005, Spring). The impact of service-learning pedagogy on faculty teaching and learning. *Michigan Journal of Community Service-Learning, 11*, 25–38. https://hdl.handle. net/2027/spo.3239521.0011.202

Stanton, T. K. (1994). The experience of faculty participants in an instructional development seminar on service-learning. *Michigan Journal of Community Service Learning, 1*(1), 7–20. http://hdl.handle.net/2027/spo.3239521.0001.101

Van Note Chism, N., Palmer, M. M., & Price, M. F. (2013). Investigating faculty development service-learning. In P. H. Clayton, R. G. Bringle, & J. A. Hatcher (Eds.), *Research on service-learning: Conceptual frameworks and assessment. Volume 2A: Students and faculty* (pp. 187–214). Stylus.

Welch, M., & Plaxton-Moore, S. (2017). Faculty development for advancing community engagement in higher education: Current trends and future directions. *Journal of Higher Education Outreach and Engagement, 21*(2), 131–166 https://openjournals.libs.uga.edu/jheoe/article/view/1333/1330

Wiggins, G. P., McTighe, J., Kiernan, L. J., Frost, F., & Association for Supervision and Curriculum Development. (1998). *Understanding by design.* Stylus.

# EIGHT

# Conclusion

I N 2021, L UCY TAUGHT A course for dual-enrollment students (those simultaneously enrolled in high school and college coursework) with a critical service-learning (CSL) focus. This work turned out to be fraught on a variety of levels, from the pandemic and logistics concerns to politics. Lucy, as the professor for the course, often found herself thinking: "Well, this is a weird semester. I'll be able to facilitate these projects the way they are *supposed to be* next semester."

But that's the thing: Teaching and learning will never be the way they are *supposed to be*, at least if one is interested in doing the work to build toward a more just world. There will also be barriers from administrations to the global pandemics. This conclusion seems like a constructive place to discuss those obstacles and imagine how the lessons that have come from the past couple of years might not hamstring us as CSL educators but embolden us.

## Online CSL

In 2020 and 2021, many colleges and universities moved to online, hybrid, flex, or some other mode of delivery as a result of the COVID-19 pandemic. For CSL, these changes have caused a particular set of problems because so much of our work is face-to-face.

There are CSL projects that can happen online. Even pre-pandemic, Heather worked with a community partner who made sleeping mats from reused grocery bags and distributed them to individuals living in transition in the university's vicinity. Heather's students could easily collect bags and make the mats on their own and could even distribute them without ever having to go to the community partner site. During the pandemic, these sleeping mats were especially important as a tent city developed between the city and the highway, a result of COVID-related evictions. Additionally, prison outreach has primarily moved online during the pandemic because there are limited opportunities for face-to-face interactions. There are book drives and letter-writing opportunities, however. With her dual-enrollment group, who, as high school students, were limited to on-campus activities during the pandemic, Lucy engaged students in community mapping activities entirely digitally using Google Maps and other online research and resources. The dual-enrollment students also formed relationships with community partners via email and Zoom calls; they were able to plan and coordinate projects, even though they could not be in these spaces in person.

Many college courses used hybrid and flex models as the pandemic progressed as well; it's likely that some of the changes to more flexible models will remain with us in higher education. Hybrid and flex classroom settings offer additional options for some in-person interactions, as safety allows. When weather allows, some CSL-oriented activities and projects can take place outdoors, for example.

Teaching any courses during the pandemic has reminded us that our students are in need of compassion and support and even more so now as the rift between the haves and the have-nots has gotten wider. Traditional college students are coping with mental and physical health concerns; nontraditional college students, which includes many community college students, are also grappling with childcare and employment. One way of building capacity for empathy is to practice empathy with our students. Modeling this empathy helps them to practice it in return.

Empathy for students during a pandemic is challenging work; we have both struggled with an increased workload, a need for extensions and leniency with our students, and our own mental and physical health needs throughout this year. Being empathetic doesn't mean that we don't set boundaries with our students and our work lives, but it does mean avoiding deficit mindsets and avoiding tropes, like blaming students for problems and mistakes. In times of struggle with our work and our students, we are inspired and affirmed by Freire's words (1970): "Because love is an act of courage, not of fear, love is a commitment to others. No matter where the oppressed are found, the act of love is commitment to their cause—the cause of liberation" (p. 89).

## CSL and Politics

In addition to a global pandemic, the new decade (2020) ushered in a host of social justice issues that emanated from the United States outward. In May, George Floyd was murdered by police officers, a moment that reverberated through the country, resulting in protests and outcries that had been bubbling for decades, if not centuries. It's 2021, and we still haven't seen the necessary reforms and reallocations that are needed to create safer lives for Black and Indigenous people. Plus, due to the political polarization that has seized the United States during the Trump presidency and continues under Biden, public discourse is often frantic.

For those of us engaged with critical theory, who have critiqued the White supremacist and capitalist ideologies that permeate schools and culture, to see White supremacists argue about "fake news" and rail against the "facts" and liberal ideologies taught in schools, it's dizzying. We have critiqued the way political ideologies infiltrate knowledge in order to maintain the status quo; they are making similar arguments but with a set of facts disassociated from empirical reality. How do we as critical educators help students understand the website for the U.S. Centers for Disease Control and Prevention? It's not a political void, but it's also not made up by a secret cabal. It's tricky and, in truth, probably the topic for another book.

But we'd be remiss not to engage with these public discourses that are certain to impact CSL projects, students, faculty, and community partners over the coming months and years. As we type, local school boards are erupting into chaos over the concept of critical race theory. How will we talk to stakeholders about critical service-learning?

## Navigating Tricky Conversations Through CSL

We have a few bits of advice, based on years of experience working in urban, rural, and suburban schools and colleges in the U.S. South.

*Be Transparent.* We gain nothing from hedging. Our goal is social change that is desperately needed, considering that we live in a time more socioeconomically polarized than at any other point in history. The work we do actually benefits those who are sometimes unable to frame it: Poor White people have been inculcated into a sort of tribalism around Whiteness, that tribalism benefits the wealthy class, not the poor White people, who continue to lack access to health care, education, and other social necessities. It may be that we are accused of liberalism. So be it. Our progressive stances include them, too.

*Be Loud.* Not by talking over marginalized folks, of course. But we should speak clearly and frequently about the work we, our students, and our community partners are doing. This discourse needs to happen on our campuses and in our communities. When people know about the work we are doing, they can also participate in the discourse. When they don't know, it's easy enough for CSL to be absorbed into political polemics.

*Be Loving.* CSL flourishes when faculty, students, and community partners are able to empathize with others, despite differences. One of our premises in this book is that facilitating empathy with our students is part of the path forward. The same is true when we interact with critics.

*Be Courageous.* A great woman once said that haters are gonna hate, hate, hate, but I just wanna do CSL—or something like that. It's true that we sometimes have to compromise and be incrementalistic in our thinking in order to progress, but it's also true that doing so doesn't mean stopping work toward and advocating for big changes. Whether from a place of ignorance or self-interest, people who oppose CSL and other progressive pedagogies are not going to offer us grace, even if we mitigate our work and our thinking. All we can do is represent ourselves honestly, do the best we can to show up for our community partners and our students while caring for our own needs, and continue doing the work that needs to be done.

So, to conclude, this work is not easy, but it is necessary. It is not straightforward, and it is messy. We return to Brameld (1965/2000), who theorizes that when society is in a state of crisis, the role of education becomes innovation and modifying; CSL offers a conduit for challenging college students to consider and work toward a socially just society. By providing a rationale for using CSL as a curriculum and pedagogy and offering a model for how faculty might engage in CSL in 2- and 4-year colleges and universities, we hope to foster the type of empathy necessary to overcome challenges and work toward equality.

### References

Brameld, T. (2000). *Education as power.* Caddo Gap Press. (Original work published 1965)

Freire, P. (1970). *Pedagogy of the oppressed.* Seabury Press.

# ◌₰ Critical Service-Learning Implementation Model

| Observable Characteristic | Present | Not Present |
| --- | --- | --- |
| **Pedagogy: The planning and preparation of the activities, lessons, and space** | | |
| **Evidence of reciprocal learning** about difference and similarity (the instructor, students, and community partner learn about each other's culture and experience) | | |
| **Instructor demonstration of understanding of student experience/ background** by referencing knowledge and making connections | | |
| **Strategically crafted activities** to learn more about student and community partner experience/background | | |
| **Student engagement in guided and open-ended reflection** | | |
| **Instructor-, community partner-, and student-selected texts/ experiences/opportunities** that spark reflection on identity development | | |
| **Evidence instructor embraces the "progressive and liberal agenda"** that undergirds critical service-learning practice (Butin, 2006[1]) | | |
| **An obvious attempt to raise critical consciousness** (Freire, 1970[2]) | | |
| **Collaborative informal and formal planning** | | |
| **Opportunities for dialogue, reflection, and writing assignments that encourage analysis** of real-world concerns and push students to consider the systemic causes | | |
| **Opportunities for students to physically explore the community** around the school/university/service setting and reflect on noticings | | |
| **Inclusion of presentations/co-teaching by community partners/ parents/stakeholders** | | |
| **Use and encouragement of careful language that promotes asset-based perspectives** | | |
| **Notes:** | | |
| **Curriculum: Classroom Activities/Discussions/Lessons: These components are present in the actual interactions in the classroom.** | | |
| **Defining Injustice** (might also be transposed with inequity/unfairness/ injustice/discrimination/bias/prejudice) | | |
| **Reframing** requires the teacher or student to imagine themselves from another perspective | | |

| Observable Characteristic | Present | Not Present |
|---|---|---|
| **Questioning** the distribution of power would include having students to think about how the world would look if there was an equal distribution of money and resources | | |
| **Clarifying** privilege might include activities like the privilege walk and poverty simulation, classroom discussions about how people are born with certain privileges | | |
| **Developing** authentic relationships among students, faculty, and partners. The teachers and students both exhibit comfort with each other in the discussion of difficult topics like race, poverty, sexuality. | | |
| **Challenging** assumptions might be demonstrated with students and teachers asking the question, "Why do you believe this?" or offering a counterperspective | | |
| **Focusing** on social justice issues that are personal to the group. There are a variety of these, but the most common are poverty, race, color, language, sexuality, orientation, gender, trafficking, DACA, religious freedom. | | |
| **Posing** questions that might challenge students' understanding of their experience and understanding of the world | | |
| **Analyzing** texts (informative and literary) for social issues (critical literacy) | | |
| **Pointing out** power structures/hierarchies | | |
| **Confronting** assumptions and stereotypes | | |
| **Accepting and Admitting** that sometimes privilege is a part of circumstance and that some people benefit from circumstances they had no control over (i.e., skin color, income of parents) | | |
| **Reflecting and Writing** about the ways in which mindsets/opinions may have changed due to knowledge gained through experience | | |
| Notes: | | |
| **Space: What does the space of the classroom look like? What are the classroom dynamics?** | | |
| **Opportunities for small group and partner discussion** | | |
| **Flexible Seating** includes nontraditional classroom furniture, easily moved desks, outdoor space | | |
| **Mutuality** (Teacher as learner and learner as teacher) | | |
| **Trust/Safety** (The teacher has established an environment where it is obvious students feel comfortable challenging their assumptions and speaking openly about difficult topics. Students share personal information and thoughts even in the presence of an observer. Everyone feels "safe.") | | |
| **Respect** (Regardless of differences of opinion, students speak to their mind and respect peers' opinions.) | | |
| **Acknowledgement and acceptance** of difference as a benefit | | |

| Observable Characteristic | Present | Not Present |
|---|---|---|
| **Opportunity** for disequilibrium/discomfort | | |
| **Mutual understanding of goals** (Within lessons and activities, the students appear to understand what is expected of them and the teacher looks to the students to help develop goals.) | | |
| **Fluidity/Flexibility** Within the learning environment, students have the opportunity to change their minds about topics/opinions without worrying they will fall behind. Students understand that they must always have a backup plan. | | |
| Notes: | | |
| **Observable Student Behaviors: Practices and Habits Exhibited by Students Participating in Critical Service-Learning** | | |
| Small-group and paired **discussion.** | | |
| **Identification** of issues of concern within community/society | | |
| Development of functional and comprehensive definition of **agency** and **activism** with real world application | | |
| **Grappling** with multiple perspectives | | |
| **Challenging** established beliefs and/or accepted "norms" | | |
| **Developing** arguments using textual evidence | | |
| **Creating** solutions/programs/education to advocate for a cause | | |
| **Acting** on evidence to create change | | |
| **Presenting** findings/research to a group/groups of stakeholders, community partners, and/or decision-makers | | |
| **Notes:** | | |

## Notes

1. Butin, D. (2006). The limits of service-learning in higher education. *Review of Higher Education, 29*(4), 473–498. https://doi.org/10.1353/rhe.2006.0025

2. Freire, P. (1970). *Pedagogy of the oppressed.* Seabury Press.

# ∾ The Legacy Project

THE LEGACY PROJECT IS A course-based service project designed to benefit community partners associated with LBST 2301: Citizenship and Education. Students start thinking about the legacy project early in the semester, and they may work on it over the course of the entire semester. First, students conduct a formal needs assessment with the community partner and map community resources and limitations in order to develop a more complete picture of why the organization exists or how a school could benefit from a service project. Upon completion of these two activities, the service-learning student will work either individually or in small groups to collaborate with the community partner in the planning and implementation of a program or project that meets the need or raises awareness about the need.

In preparation for exiting the service partnership each semester, the student must show evidence of communication with the community partner/representative. This may come in the form of a Google document where the project is planned with insight from community partner, or it may include screenshots of emails between student(s) and the community partner. Regardless, students must demonstrate open lines of communication in developing this project.

Students must also provide evidence that they have conducted research into the issue/problem causing the need for this organization. In the final upload of the project, students will include links to or examples of texts/articles/websites that you used to research possible solutions to the problem and the potential impact.

Upon completion of the service project, students will use the planning form and project outline to write a reflection paper addressing the learning associated with the project and demonstrating a solid grasp of critical service-learning must be submitted with the completed Legacy Project to round out this assignment.

Examples of Legacy Projects completed in this course include the following:

- A spaghetti dinner fundraiser for Room in the Inn at University City Church (UCC).[1] Through this fundraiser, students in LBST 2301 raised money to be donated to support the needs of Room in the Inn over several semesters. University of North Carolina Charlotte (UNCC) students participating in this project have either purchased the food or relied on community donations and prepared the meals that are sold to diners (generally, the cost is about $5, but donations are accepted). The event, held in the UCC gym is open to the public and tickets are either pre-sold or purchased at the door. Proceeds from the dinner to go Room in the Inn to purchase necessary supplies to run the temporary housing from December to March each year.

- Summer Reading Program at University City Elementary School that built on the survey results of teachers at the school from the previous semester. Students who implemented this legacy project collected books and created reading logs and reading resources for parents and students. SL students gave all Reading Program students in second grade a canvas bag full of books (appropriate to their reading levels), reading logs, stickers, and resources for parents. These logs will be turned into the school for prizes at the end of the summer.

- Introduction to The Responsible Change Project Module for eighth graders at University City Middle School. Students in LBST 2301 created a Google Drive folder with materials related to the research/service project conducted by students in eighth-grade English language arts classes. This introductory module includes resources to help with calling local organizations and representatives, writing professional emails, and a video of previous eighth graders and their teachers explaining the outcomes of the project.

## Alignment With Course Learning Objectives

**Critical Thinking:** Students will be able to define or develop a problem/question/approach appropriate in a given field of inquiry, evaluate and analyze evidence that is relevant to that problem, and then assemble evidence to generate valid and defensible conclusions.

**Communication:** Students will be able to present content in a way that conveys/creates meaning for a given purpose and audience and is consistent with the conventions appropriate for a given communicative context.

**Students will also:**

- Be able to define service-learning and critical service-learning.
- Articulate the differences between community service, volunteerism, and service-learning.
- Develop an operational definition of global education.
- Identify critical issues relating to urban education in the U.S.
- Explain the need for community organizations.
- Examine the impact of educational policies on schools, children, and families.
- Identify both the educational limitations and opportunities for young people.
- Work with K–12 students at schools or community sites to gain experience and develop firsthand understanding of challenges and possibilities of education.
- Explore how businesses, organizations, and community support the needs of the underserved student population.

The Legacy Project aligns with all the learning objectives for the course through the multiple steps that students take in developing the project:

- Community Partner Needs Assessment
- Physical Community Mapping
- Community Mapping Analysis
- Legacy Project Proposal
- Legacy Project Speed Crowdsourcing
- Legacy Project Rubric

Over the years, this project has had several iterations, and as a result, there is no established format for what the project looks like. There are several examples of Legacy Projects students have completed in the section above, and there are also examples (i.e., video introduction to the Responsible Change Project at University City Middle School) provided in the Legacy Project Module on Canvas. In the last 8 weeks of the semester, students will complete a Community Partner Needs Assessment, develop a proposal based on those needs, take the proposal through the peer review process, and implement or execute the Legacy Project. Students have to become comfortable with the fact that there is no established format for this Legacy Project; however, they must show the following over the course of the development of the project:

**Legacy Project Presentations will occur on [insert date] with each group presenting their Legacy Project in the form of a Google slideshow. Each slideshow must include the following elements:**

- Slide 1: Title of Legacy Project and Group Member Names
- Slide 2: Explain the approach you used in the development of your Legacy Project. The approach, question or problem statement is clear, insightful, explicit and situated within a field of inquiry. (The problem statement comes directly from the Mapping the Community Assignment and the group's unofficial needs assessment and communication with the community partner).
- Slide 3: Explain the process you used for developing the Legacy Project. How did you develop this idea? What were the ideas that were adopted and what are the others that might have been scrapped for lack of time or lack of resources?
- Slide 4: What is the actual Legacy Project? What have you done or will you do to benefit your community partner? What evidence do you have of the work you have already done?
- Slide 5: What was the timeline for the project? Has it been completed? When do you expect to complete this phase of the project?
- Slide 6: How might this project be continued in the course for the next semester? In what ways do you imagine next semester's class can build on this project?
- Slide 7: What feedback from the online discussion forum and readings from the course influenced the development of your Legacy Project?
- Slide 8: Who, outside of this class was responsible for helping your group develop your project? In other words, who would you thank?
- Slide 9: Any citations from outside sources.
- Requirement: Uses conventions appropriate for a given communicative context in a comprehensive and sophisticated manner. (Polish of the project is assessed as a component of the rubric; conventions and audience must be considered.)

The link to this slideshow, created in Google Slides, must be uploaded to the Canvas assignment by [insert deadline]. All presentations will be loaded at the beginning of class on Tuesday morning. Each group will have 10 minutes to present during our last class. Each group will also have 2 minutes to field questions and provide answers from the class. Please treat this as a professional presentation and prepare your order of speaking and what you will say ahead of time.

UPLOAD Legacy Project Slideshow.

## Note

1. All place names have been changed for privacy.

# ❦ Community Mapping Project

ALL LEARNERS MAY CHOOSE TO work with 1–2 partners (pairs/trios) during this assignment. Individual reflection should be completed autonomously.

The purpose of this project is to identify community assets and needs. The primary objective is to collect data in order to create a map of community assets and resources within a defined area. A community map highlights people, physical structures, organizations, and institutions that can be utilized to support students and their families.

Rationale: Community mapping is an essential, yet often overlooked, step in the planning process for meaningful community engagement. Creating contact lists and physical maps of nearby institutions and associations enables teachers and other school personnel to visualize the unique assets that are present in the communities in which they work. Identifying and mapping these assets will reinforce the topic that is under investigation or perhaps lead to new inquiries and learning opportunities.

**Project Components:**

1. Define and analyze a geographic area of interest in order to highlight the people, physical structures, organizations, and institutions within the community.
2. Using Google Maps or Scribble Maps (see the tutorial on the website), zoom into your location/community. Circumscribe the "zone" around the school that includes the communities in which students who attend the school live.
3. Annotate the map using the tools on your computer. Insert graphics, captions, and nearby places of interest, OR take a screen shot of the area on a map and annotate it using the tools in PowerPoint or Google Slides. Annotate (add to the map) or highlight (point out on the map) the following:
   - Essential services
   - Essential retail outlets (groceries, pharmacies)

- Local associations
  - An association is a group of citizens joined together around a common goal that benefits the overall community.
- Local institutions in the community.
  - Institutions are organizations that can be public, private or non-profit and include local businesses, schools, parks, libraries, police stations, social service agencies, community colleges, and hospitals.
4. Talk with someone who might be aware of other community resources that are difficult to locate on a map. Examples of individuals you might interview include school social worker, counselors, school nurse, administrator, teacher or teacher assistant who lives in the community or who has worked at the organization/school for an extended period, coaches, band or chorus teachers, parent/teacher organization officers, booster club members, parents of students, students and themselves.

Questions to ask include:

- Are there groups and organizations active in the community of which I might not be aware?
- Are there community organizations that serve this school of which I might not be aware?
- Note: You are not seeking organizations within the school (student-based clubs, etc.) but those outside the school that support this school or its community.

Deliverables:

1. **Create a presentation** that *highlights the community's assets* and identifies its *strengths and weaknesses.* Using a presentation tool (i.e., PowerPoint, Google Slides, Prezi, etc.) create a presentation that includes the following:
   - Annotated Map
   - Demographics of the community
     - NOTE: Remember our writing about race and ethnicity as you identify varied groups in the community.

- Assets in the community
  - Describe at least three (3) places/groups/organizations that you consider to be assets in this community or identify 8-10 public resources (bus lines, community parks, farmers markets) within a 10-minute drive that you can use either individually or as a class.
  - These may be specific places/organizations identified on your annotated map . . .
  - OR organizations/resources that serve the community but don't have a specific geographical location (e.g., fraternal organizations)
- Strengths
  - What general strengths of this community has your research uncovered?
  - What does the community offer to those who do not live there?
- Weaknesses
  - What supports do you perceive this community to be lacking?
  - What might outsiders (to the community) experience (positively or negatively) by being a part of your community?
  - In what way is your community welcoming to outsiders?

2. **Write OR Record an Individual Reflection** about what you learned during this assignment. **Connect your reflection to the course content by referencing 2 or more course readings/resources**. This reflection should be 3–5 pages, double-spaced (avoid large gaps between sections/paragraphs), and should address the following:
   - What did you learn through completing this project in terms of analyzing a community?
   - How has completing this project impacted the way you think about the community/your students' access to the community?
   - What connections can you make to the texts/content of the course? Reference at least TWO readings/course content.
   - How does this project impact the way you view yourself as a member of the community?

*Before submitting your Community Mapping project, conduct a self-assessment using the rubric provided and make sure you have included each required component. You do **not** need to submit evidence of this self-assessment.*

# Traditional vs. Critical Service-Learning

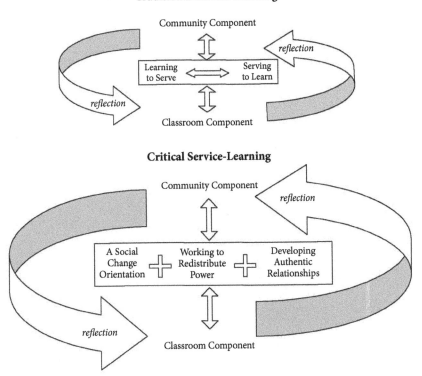

Reprinted with permission from Mitchell, T.D. (2008). Traditional vs. critical service-learning: Engaging the literature to differentiate two models: *Michigan Journal of Community Service-Learning*, Spring, 50–65.

# About the Authors

**Dr. Heather Coffey** is a professor in the Department of Middle, Secondary and K–12 Education and serves as the director of the University of North Carolina at Charlotte Writing Project. Dr. Coffey's primary teaching responsibilities include graduate English language arts methods as well as service-learning courses. Her research interests include ways to develop critical literacy with urban learners, bridging the gap between educational theory and practice in teacher education, and supporting in-service teachers in urban school settings through professional development. Dr. Coffey's record of publication includes book chapters and articles in refereed practitioner and research journals. She is currently investigating the ways in which urban learners can develop agency through research and writing and work for social justice in their communities.

**Lucy Arnold** is an assistant professor of English at Limestone University, where she also coordinates the English education program. She earned her PhD in curriculum and instruction and her MA in English education from the University of North Carolina (UNC) at Charlotte. Her BA in English was awarded by the University of South Carolina. Lucy has been a member of the National Writing Project (NWP) since 2002 and has been a part of the NWP leadership team at UNC–Charlotte for years. She has published articles in state and national publications, including the *English Journal* and *Radical Teacher*. She teaches coursework on literacy, assessment, American literature, and writing. In her spare time, she reads and listens to a number of podcasts; she also runs, practices yoga, bakes, and plays video games.

# Index